Maria Sibylla Merian
ARTIST | SCIENTIST | ADVENTURER

Sarah B. Pomeroy
and Jeyaraney Kathirithamby

The J. Paul Getty Museum • Los Angeles

To my grandchildren, Nate, Joel, Jesse, Talia, Simone, Dina, and Jacob; to the memory of Alexandra Pomeroy; and to the memory of Elicia Brown Pomeroy
⁓SBP

To Jacob Arun
⁓JK

Lobster Claw with Potter Wasp and Southern Army Worm from *The Insects of Surinam* by Maria Sibylla Merian

Contents

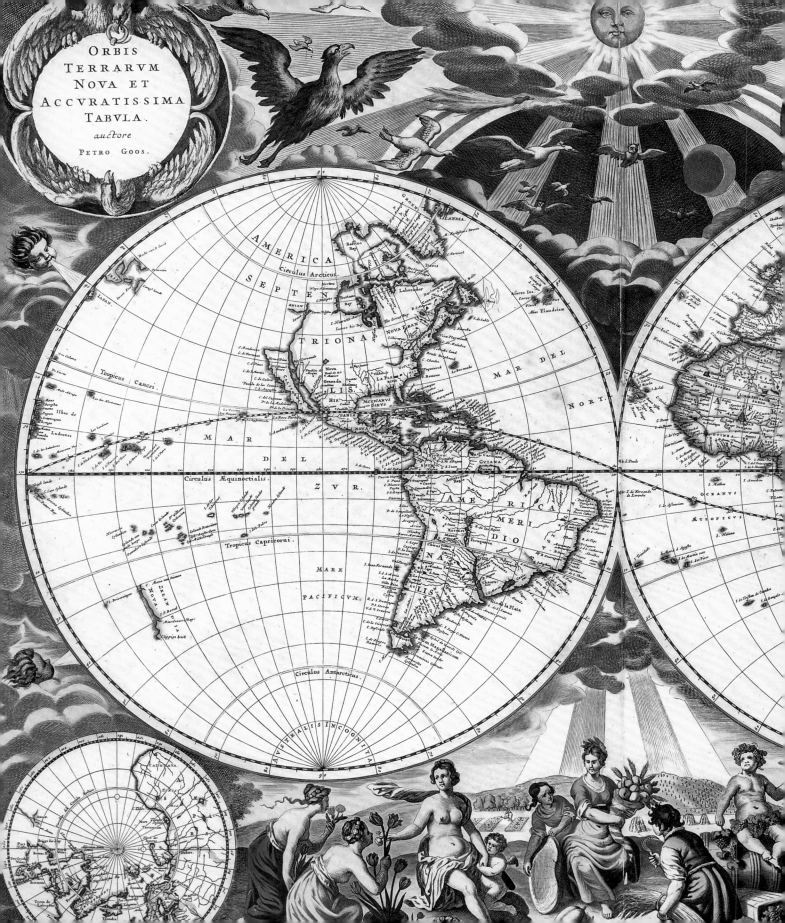

Nieuwe
WERELT KAERT
uyt gegeven
tot AMSTELDAM *by*
Pieter Goos.

Introduction

"All this inspired me to undertake a long
and costly journey, and to sail to Surinam in America."

    Maria Sibylla Merian

It was a dangerous voyage—two months crossing the Atlantic Ocean in a wooden boat about the
length of two school buses. Storms rocked the seas,
and pirates plied the waters looking for ships carrying valuable cargo. Friends begged Maria Sibylla
Merian not to go, but she refused to listen to them.
She had made up her mind.

In June 1699 Maria Sibylla and her daughter
Dorothea sailed from Holland to Surinam, in South
America, to explore the jungles in search of exotic
creatures no European had ever seen. They were the
first people to journey to the Americas for purely scientific reasons, and they planned to study and paint
pictures of every new animal and insect they found.

Maria Sibylla Merian was one of the earliest
entomologists—scientists who study insects—and
also one of the world's first ecologists—scientists
who study the relationships among living things in
the environment. At the age of thirteen she began an
important study of metamorphosis, the process by

which caterpillars change into moths and butterflies. She investigated the development of tadpoles into frogs and was the first to describe army ants, orb weaver spiders, and many other rain-forest creatures. She understood how living things interacted and was the first to draw a complex ecosystem on a single page. More than a dozen species of insects, animals, and plants have been named in her honor.

Not only a scientist, Maria Sibylla Merian was also a famous artist. She had a talent for making accurate illustrations of plants and animals that were also very beautiful. She pictured insects among the flowers and fruits they liked to eat, and she did so in artistic ways that were wonderful to see. Today, paintings, drawings, and hand-colored books by Maria Sibylla Merian can be found in museums and art collections all over the world.

Artist, scientist, adventurer: Maria Sibylla Merian, born in 1647, more than 350 years ago, was a woman far ahead of her time.

1719 edition of *The Insects of Surinam* by Maria Sibylla Merian, now in the collection of the Getty Research Institute in Los Angeles, California

Coral Bean Tree with Giant Silkworm from *The Insects of Surinam* by Maria Sibylla Merian

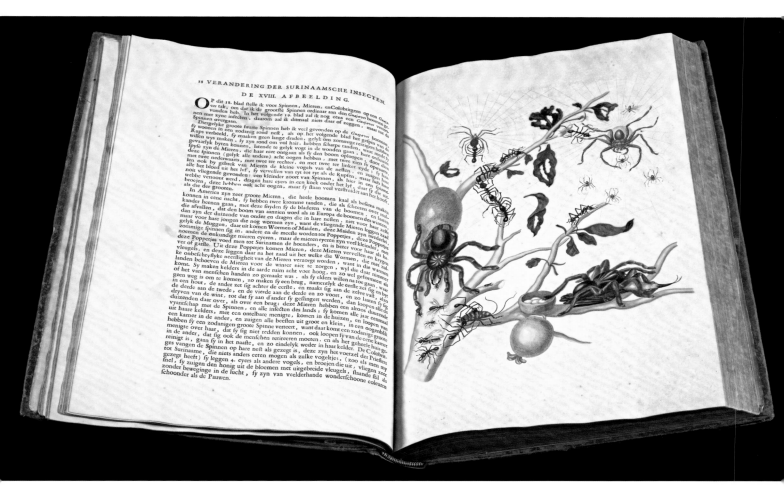

Chapter one
Growing Up with Art and Nature

"This inspired me to collect all the caterpillars I could find and to observe their metamorphoses."

— *Maria Sibylla Merian*

Stories of faraway places, paintings of flowers, and a family of artists surrounded Maria Sibylla Merian as she grew up. Her extended family was huge, including half brothers, half sisters, and stepsisters, and her home in Frankfurt, Germany, was always filled with people. The painting studio was her favorite room in the house, cluttered with brushes, easels, dried flowers, and paints in many colors. It was a busy place, where students and apprentices came to study with her stepfather, Jacob Marrel. Jacob was a well-known painter of flowers woven into wreaths or arranged in vases. This type of painting is called still life, because it shows objects captured in a moment, as if frozen in time. As long as she didn't get in the way, young Maria Sibylla was allowed in the studio. She watched the artists at work and helped by cleaning brushes and mixing paints.

When Jacob realized that Maria Sibylla was good at drawing, he began to include her in the lessons he gave to his students. She learned to paint in her own home, which was lucky, because girls were not allowed to attend art school. And unlike Jacob's male students, Maria Sibylla could not become an apprentice in another artist's studio. But she could still hope to become a professional artist someday, and she learned all she could from her artistic family.

Maria Sibylla's father, Matthäus Merian the Elder, had been an artist and publisher. He had children from his first marriage before he married Maria Sibylla's mother, Johanna Sibylla Heim. Maria Sibylla's father died when she was only three years old. Her mother later married Jacob Marrel, who also had children from his first marriage. Maria Sibylla learned about art from her stepfather, her half

Iris with Dot Moth from *The Caterpillar Book* by Maria Sibylla Merian

View of Frankfurt in a Floral Wreath by Jacob Marrel, 1650–51

Maria Sibylla's stepfather, Jacob Marrel, was a well-known artist, and he painted this wreath of flowers. In the center he shows a miniature view of the city where the family lived, along the Main River in Germany.

Floral Wreath with Lilies, Anemones, Peonies, and a Sunflower from *The Caterpillar Book* by Maria Sibylla Merian

Maria Sibylla learned to paint from her stepfather, and when she was grown-up, she often painted wreaths of flowers like the ones her step-father made in his art studio.

Oil Painting Studio printed by Theodor Galle, about 1580, after a design by Jan van der Straet

Artists' studios were busy places. In this picture the master artist is standing on a platform painting a large canvas, while apprentices and assistants work all around him. On the left, one paints the portrait of a live model who sits in a chair nearby. Two apprentices are sketching. In the center, a young man is mixing colors, while in the background, on the right, two others are grinding pigments and mixing them with oil to make paint.

Roman Denarius with Sibylla, mint of Rome, 65 BCE

Maria's middle name, Sibylla, is derived from the name of an ancient Roman prophet, Sibyl of Cumae, who was said to tell the future. She is depicted on this Roman coin made about two thousand years ago. Roman history and mythology were popular in Europe during the seventeenth century.

Portrait of the Family of Matthäus Merian the Elder by Matthäus Merian the Younger, 1642

This is a portrait of Maria Sibylla's father, the artist Matthäus Merian the Elder, surrounded by his first wife and their children. The painting shows that Maria Sibylla was born into a large family, including half siblings who were much older than she was. The figure on the left is Matthäus Merian the Younger, who was also an artist and points himself out as the one who painted this picture. Some of the family members are dressed up like ancient Romans, whom they admired. The child on the right is holding a plaster cast of the head of an enormous Roman statue. Artists used these casts as models for their paintings.

brothers, and the many artists who visited or worked in Jacob's studio. Besides drawing, painting, and engraving, she learned to see like an artist, to develop her skills at observation, and to think like artists do about the world around them.

Like most artists of her time, Maria Sibylla probably began by copying drawings and paintings made by others. Since her stepfather's workshop specialized in flower paintings, she may have started with small sketches of individual flowers before she tried putting them together in larger compositions. Some of her later paintings feature single flowers, and some are like Jacob's, with vases filled with many flowers that would have bloomed at different times of the year.

Jacob painted his flowers with watercolors on vellum—a sheet of animal skin, scraped thin, soaked in lime, and stretched and dried. Vellum was expensive, and not a bit was wasted. In the studio Maria Sibylla learned how to prepare vellum with a thin coating of opaque white material that created a bright, smooth base for the watercolor paints that had been so carefully prepared.

Yellow for daffodils, pink for carnations, blue for irises . . . these colors did not come in trays or tubes as they do today. Artists like Maria Sibylla had to make their own paints using natural materials, including minerals, plants, and even shellfish and insects. These were ground into powders called pigments. Many came from

Vase with Flowers by Jacob Marrel, 1635

Maria Sibylla's stepfather painted this arrangement of flowers. There are insects and animals in the painting too, but they lack detail and seem out of place on top of a wooden table.

Spring Flowers in a Chinese Vase from *The New Book of Flowers* by Maria Sibylla Merian

Maria Sibylla painted this still life. She included the stag beetle to "enliven" the painting, which was mainly focused on the flowers. In her later work, Maria Sibylla showed insects in their natural environments.

Self-Portrait by Jacob Marrel, 1635

After the death of Maria Sibylla's father, her mother married the artist Jacob Marrel. In this self-portrait he shows himself at the age of twenty-one, painting one of the floral still lifes for which he was best known.

Cochineal, Lapis Lazuli, and Gum Arabic

These are some of the natural materials Maria Sibylla used to make paints.

Study Book by Maria Sibylla Merian

When she was thirteen, Maria Sibylla began to record her observations about caterpillars and butterflies, and she painted pictures of them in full color. She later copied her notes into a study book she would keep nearly all her life. It eventually included 318 studies of different insects and hundreds of drawings of eggs, pupae, caterpillars, beetles, butterflies, moths, and other creatures. She wrote in German using black letter, or Gothic script, common throughout Europe in the seventeenth century but today read only by scholars.

faraway lands: orange-red cinnabar from Spain, blue lapis lazuli stone from Afghanistan. Carmine red came all the way from South America, where it was made from cochineal insects that live only on a particular type of cactus. To use these pigments, Maria Sibylla first had to mix them with a binder, something that made them stick to the vellum. Oils were used for oil paints, but to make watercolors, Maria Sibylla mixed the pigments with water and gum arabic, a sticky substance collected from the bark of acacia trees. It wasn't easy to get just the right mix of pigments to match the exact color of a particular flower, or to get just the right amount of binder to make the color easy to paint with and to dry—but not too fast. Maria Sibylla learned by doing.

There were not just flowers but also insects in some of Jacob's paintings, and in the studio there were dead, dried specimens stuck on pins for the artists to use as models. As Maria Sibylla later recalled, "I was always encouraged to embellish my flower painting with caterpillars, summer birds [butterflies] and such little animals in the same manner in which landscape painters do in pictures, to enliven the one through the other, so to speak." But Maria Sibylla didn't want to use dead bugs as models; she wanted to paint insects while they were alive, to capture their true colors and show how they behaved in their natural environments. She was curious about their lives—where they came from and how they grew. She especially loved to watch wiggling silkworms and the changes they went through from egg to larva to cocoon to moth. "Then I noticed that much more beautiful butterflies and moths emerged from other caterpillars," she wrote. "This inspired me to collect all the caterpillars I could find and to observe their metamorphoses." Metamorphosis is a Greek word meaning "transformation." The word could apply to Maria Sibylla herself, as she went through many changes during the course of her adventurous life.

The first transformation took place at age thirteen, when she made a surprising decision. "I set aside my social life. I devoted all my time to these observations [of insects] and to improving my abilities in the art of painting, so that I could both draw individual specimens and paint them as they were in nature. I collected all the insects I could find around Frankfurt . . . and painted them very precisely on vellum."

The Reeling of Silk printed by Karel van Mallery, about 1595, after a design by Jan van der Straet

Silk manufacture was women's work. In this engraving the woman holding a child is supervising the workshop. The women pictured in the background are gathering cocoons to be brought indoors. Inside, other women unwind the silk fibers from the cocoons and wind them onto reels so that they can be spun into thread.

Wreath of White Mulberry with Silkworm Metamorphosis from *The Caterpillar Book* by Maria Sibylla Merian

On this decorative page Maria Sibylla depicted the silkworm in different stages of development on a wreath made with its favorite food—mulberry leaves.

Maria Sibylla collected caterpillars and insects from gardens within walking distance of her home. She found specimens in trees along the river and took rides in a horse-drawn carriage to the countryside just beyond the city. To her mother's dismay, she began raising caterpillars at home, keeping them alive in wooden boxes and giving them lettuce leaves to eat. She watched each one change from a caterpillar to a moth or butterfly. Like a modern scientist, she took notes, recording her observations with words, drawings, and paintings. Careful note-taking was a habit she would keep throughout her life.

She continued to study silkworms, which she considered "the most useful and noble of all worms and caterpillars" because the fibers of their cocoons could be made into silk cloth. She would not have found silkworms outside but at a silk manufacturer's workshop. The ancient Chinese had been the first to spin silk thread from the fibers of the silkworm cocoon, and the fabrics they wove were the envy of the world. The women of ancient Rome loved silks for their lightness and the way they absorbed colorful dyes. But for a long time no one knew how to make silk outside of China, and the Chinese emperors threatened death to anyone who would

Metamorphosis of the Silkworm

Maria Sibylla's first illustration in her first scientific book was the life cycle of the silkworm, which she based on the earliest observations in her study book. The life cycle begins with the eggs (lower right corner), which hatch into caterpillars (technically called larvae) after ten days. The bodies of caterpillars are segmented and often covered with hairs. As a caterpillar eats, it grows and periodically sheds its outer skin—which is actually an external skeleton called a cuticle—in a process called molting. Maria Sibylla wrote, "The size of the larvae increases every day, especially when they have enough food. They reach their full size in several weeks to two months. The larvae shed their skins completely three or four times, just as a person pulls off a shirt over his head." The silkworm caterpillar sheds its cuticle five times. The large caterpillar in the lower middle of the picture is sitting on a mulberry leaf, and it is in the process of shedding its wrinkled cuticle. A cuticle that has already been shed is to the left of the mulberry leaf.

In the next stage of metamorphosis, the caterpillar uses its silk glands to produce a fluid that it forces through its mouth. This fluid hardens in the air to create the silk thread that it wraps or spins around its body to form a protective cocoon. Inside the cocoon, the caterpillar changes into a pupa. Maria Sibylla shows a yellow cocoon in the middle of the painting. Just above it is a cocoon showing the pupa inside, and a whole pupa is visible on the far right. While the insect is a pupa, chemical reactions cause many of the larval tissues to break down, and the pupa fills with what appears to be a white, milky sap. Then flat, round sheets of cells called imaginal discs begin to form structures such as adult wings, legs, and antennae. This process takes five to seven days. Finally the

Metamorphosis of the Silkworm from *The Caterpillar Book* by Maria Sibylla Merian

adult moth emerges, leaving the cocoon empty.

At the top are two adult moths. The male on the left is secreting semen. The female, which is much bigger, is laying eggs. Maria Sibylla showed the reproductive process because it was the least understood part of the insect life cycle at that time. Insect eggs are tiny and hard to see

without a magnifying glass, and some people didn't know they existed, thinking that worms, caterpillars, and flies simply emerged from rotten food or dirt. Maria Sibylla's careful observation of insect reproduction and her detailed diagram of metamorphosis helped to disprove these mistaken beliefs.

reveal the secret. Eventually travelers smuggled silkworms out of China, and Europeans began cultivating them, together with the mulberry trees on which they fed. By Maria Sibylla's day, silk was made in Frankfurt in family workshops not unlike the Marrel art studio.

But Maria Sibylla wasn't interested in silkworms just for their cocoons. She was fascinated by the changes that occurred throughout their life cycle. She described their appearance and behavior in her notes and drew pictures of the eggs that developed into caterpillars that spun cocoons, out of which flew moths that laid eggs that developed into caterpillars . . . it was all amazing to her. She wrote, "The metamorphosis of caterpillars has happened so many times one is full of praise at God's mysterious powers and the wonderful attention he pays to such insignificant little creatures."

Still, why would Maria Sibylla go to such trouble to observe metamorphosis firsthand, instead of reading about it in a book? Why would she want to collect worms she had to feed every day, whose boxes she had to keep clean? Because at the time, no book existed that explained insect metamorphosis correctly. Some people still believed in Aristotle's theory of "spontaneous generation," which held that living things could spring from nonliving matter. They didn't know that all insects laid eggs and thought some just "spontaneously" grew out of mud and garbage. It would take collecting the insects, raising them to adulthood, and observing their reproduction to begin to comprehend the whole process of metamorphosis. And that is exactly what Maria Sibylla started doing when she was thirteen years old.

Women's Work

In households where there was a family business to run, everybody worked, almost all the time. Men, women, children, and servants all had jobs to do and helped in whatever way they could to support the family. Still, in addition to the family business, some tasks were considered "women's work" that men were never expected to do. These included cooking, washing clothes, cleaning, sewing, and caring for children. Maria Sibylla probably had to do some of these chores at home.

A Woman Cleaning from *Five Feminine Occupations* by Geertruydt Roghman, 1640–57

The Lacemaker by Nicolaes Maes, about 1656

Portrait of Sara Marrel by Johann Andreas Graff, 1658

Maria Sibylla's stepsister Sara Marrel is shown doing embroidery in the family's workroom. She is bent over her sewing, following a design in a pattern book that lies open on the table. This picture shows some details of Maria Sibylla's home, such as the drawing instruments on the table, the artist's easel in the corner, and the clothing worn by girls in her family. Sara is dressed for work, wearing a pinafore to protect her dress and a kerchief to cover her hair. This sketch was made by one of Jacob Marrel's apprentices, Johann Andreas Graff.

Embroidered Sampler, 1691

This piece of embroidery is typical of those made by girls and women in seventeenth-century Germany. Called a sampler, it was used for trying out different kinds of decorative sewing stitches and designs. This one shows the alphabet, flowers, and fruit trees. The year 1691 can be read both right-side up and upside down.

Maria Sibylla began her study of metamorphosis in 1660, nine years before the first accurate descriptions were published in books. In 1669 Jan Swammerdam published *The Natural History of Insects* in Holland, and in Italy the same year Marcello Malpighi published *On the Silkworm*. Swammerdam and Malpighi are sometimes given credit for "discovering" metamorphosis. Though Maria Sibylla started recording her observations earlier, she would not publish her findings until 1679.

Maria Sibylla would have liked to spend all of her time studying and drawing insects and the fruits, flowers, and leaves they ate, but she had many other responsibilities in her family's busy home. Girls growing up in the seventeenth century were taught the skills they would need to raise a family and run a household. Maria Sibylla learned from her mother, whom she loved very much and stayed close to all her life. She learned to cook and to sew, as women had to make and repair their family's clothes. The girls in Maria Sibylla's house were taught the special sewing skill of embroidery, also called "needle-painting." It involved sewing colored thread onto cloth using different types of stitches to create patterns and pictures. Embroidery decorated fine table linens and clothing for men and women. Some of Maria Sibylla's early paintings of flowers were meant to be used as patterns for embroidery.

At the same time she was doing her chores and learning to be an artist, Maria Sibylla was learning to read and write, possibly from her mother or at one of the "dame schools" where educated older women taught young girls. Most girls learned at least well enough to read the Bible. Maria Sibylla also studied French and Latin

Frankfurt

Maria Sibylla's father, Matthäus Merian the Elder, engraved this view of Frankfurt, Germany—the city where he lived and where Maria Sibylla grew up. Notice the windmill, used for pumping water and grinding grain for bread. The many boats in the Main River show that Frankfurt was a busy port and center of trade. The only buildings in the picture with names written on them are churches. Religion was a big part of life in Frankfurt, and the city was home to people of many faiths, including Jews, Muslims, and Christians of different denominations.

The Merian family followed a Protestant Christian faith founded by John Calvin. Protestants "protested" certain practices of the Roman Catholic Church and broke away from it to worship separately. This historical period is called the Reformation, because old ideas about religion were being reformed, and new ways of thinking were emerging—in religion, in art, and also in science.

The City of Frankfurt by Matthäus Merian the Elder, before 1619

(the language used by scholars), probably from her parents, her half brothers, or tutors. This was unusual training for a girl at the time.

Maria Sibylla's stepfather had many books in his library, and her father, Matthäus Merian, had been a printer, publisher, and artist. Maria Sibylla had probably seen many of the beautifully illustrated books that came from the Merian publishing house. Some were nearly a foot tall and filled with pictures of distant places. One series of volumes gave views of towns and cities throughout Germany and Switzerland. They showed natural landscapes as well as buildings and streets. But even more fascinating was *Historia Americae*, later called *Grand Voyages*, which depicted stories of exploration. In the centuries after Columbus first sailed to the Americas, Europeans were fascinated by the "New World," where there were people, plants, and animals they had never seen before. Some of these were pictured in *Grand Voyages*. And perhaps, from these pictures of unfamiliar cities and a distant continent, and from the exotic colors arriving at the Marrel studio from all over the globe, the seed of an idea was planted in Maria Sibylla's mind. Maybe she even dared to dream of a life of travel and adventure.

The books from Matthäus Merian's workshop were famous throughout Europe. Maria Sibylla's two older half brothers, Matthäus the Younger and Caspar, carried on the Merian publishing business after their father died. Maria Sibylla may have visited their printing shop. Perhaps she helped them sort the metal letters that would be formed into words on a tray, spread with ink, and loaded into the printing press. She probably watched as they used sharp implements to cut designs onto

Intaglio Printmaking from *Encyclopaedia* by Denis Diderot and Jean le Rond d'Alembert, 1769

Employing the intaglio method, artists used a sharp tool to engrave a design onto a copper plate. The surface was covered in ink, and then it was wiped off so that the ink remained only in the engraved grooves. Then the plate was put into a rolling press, like this one, which pressed the inked plate against paper or vellum, leaving an imprint of the design. Notice the newly printed illustrations hanging up to dry in this printing workshop.

Columbus and His Brother Bartholomew Are Captured and Returned to Spain from *Grand Voyages*, engraved by Theodor de Bry, 1594, published by Matthäus Merian the Elder, 1634

Books from the Merian publishing house were popular with people interested in travel and adventure. In this scene from *Grand Voyages*, Christopher Columbus and his brother Bartholomew are depicted on the Caribbean island of Hispaniola (now Haiti and the Dominican Republic).

copper plates to make engravings for book illustrations. The copper plates were also spread with ink and put into the press, which imprinted the words and pictures onto vellum or paper. Then the sheets were hung to dry before they were purchased by readers who would take them to a bookbinder to be stitched between leather covers. The motto of the Merian publishing house was *Pietas contenta lucratur*, a Latin phrase meaning "industrious piety pays," a philosophy that would guide Maria Sibylla throughout her life.

Maria Sibylla's family were Calvinists, followers of John Calvin, a Protestant teacher who encouraged men and women to live simply, work hard, and prosper—as Matthäus had done with his publishing business. Instead of depicting Catholic saints and Bible stories, Protestant artists preferred to create pictures of flowers, landscapes, and ordinary people going about their everyday chores. Protestantism fostered both a questioning attitude and a confidence in human ability to solve problems. These strands of thought were part of Maria Sibylla's education.

Just before Maria Sibylla set aside her social life to study and draw caterpillars, one of her stepfather's apprentices, Johann Andreas Graff, went off to Italy to study art. Another apprentice, Abraham Mignon, remained in Frankfurt. Whenever Maria Sibylla's stepfather went on a long journey, as he often did as part of his business as an art dealer, Mignon continued her art lessons and helped her improve her ability to paint butterflies and flowers with beauty and skill.

With her art and her study of insects, her reading and her household chores, Maria Sibylla's early years were busy and full.

Chapter two
Painter, Scientist, Wife, Mother

"Wherein by means of an entirely new invention the origin, food, and development of caterpillars, worms, butterflies, moths, flies, and other such little animals . . . are diligently examined."

❧ *Maria Sibylla Merian*

Dandelion with Pale Tussock Moth from *The Caterpillar Book* by Maria Sibylla Merian

By the age of seventeen, Maria Sibylla had developed into a mature and capable young woman. She was a professionally trained artist who could draw, paint, and make engravings. She was also an excellent housekeeper and was skilled at sewing and embroidery. Like almost every young woman of her time, she expected to become a wife and a mother someday. And since the only young men she knew were apprentices in her stepfather's studio, it was no surprise when she married one of them.

She had last seen Johann Andreas Graff when she was twelve, before he left to study drawing in Rome and Venice. Now back in Frankfurt, Andreas was twenty-seven and ready to start a new life and art career. Whether he and Maria Sibylla fell in love, or made a good business arrangement, or both, the couple married the following year, in May 1665. The wedding was important enough that poems by family and friends were printed for the occasion. Afterward, the couple planned to produce art together, perhaps one day setting up a home studio like the one in which Maria Sibylla grew up. The marriage seemed to have good prospects for prosperity as well as happiness.

For the next three years the couple lived with Maria Sibylla's family and worked in her stepfather's studio. In 1668 a daughter was born, and they named her Johanna, after Maria Sibylla's mother. She would grow up in a household of artists, just like her own mother.

Even with a new baby and new responsibilities, Maria Sibylla continued to draw, paint, and study insects and plants. One of the paintings from the early years of her marriage is *Pomegranate Tree and Painted Lady Butterfly*, which is more like a diagram of the life cycle of a pomegranate than a realistic painting. It shows several stages at

Portrait of Maria Sibylla Merian by Jacob Marrel, 1679

This portrait of Maria Sibylla was made by Jacob Marrel. Maria Sibylla is presented as a mature, self-confident woman, dressed in black because a modest Protestant woman would never wear bright colors. But her expensive dress, lacy white collar, and her jewelry—necklace, earrings, and hair ornament—indicate that she is successful and prosperous.

Family Group in an Interior by Quiringh Gerritsz. van Brekelenkam, 1658–60

This painting shows a Protestant household from Maria Sibylla's era. The women are dressed in black, with lace collars like the one Maria Sibylla wears in her 1679 portrait. The family is finishing its Sunday meal before returning to church.

Pomegranate Tree and Painted Lady Butterfly by Maria Sibylla Merian, about 1665

This is one of the earliest existing paintings by Maria Sibylla. Though technically a still life, it does not present the pomegranate tree frozen at a particular moment in time. Instead, it shows several stages of pomegranate growth all at once. This early painting reveals many of Maria Sibylla's later interests—the cycles of growth and decay, the interactions of plants and insects, and the importance of showing nature in precise detail.

Egidius Square in Nuremberg by Johann Andreas Graff, 1682

Maria Sibylla's husband, whom she called Andreas, studied architectural drawing in Italy, and he specialized in city scenes. In this view of Nuremberg, his skill is visible in the ornate details of the city's buildings and even in the treatment of shadows.

once—the flower at the top, one fruit ripening on the tree and another so ripe it is splitting open, and finally, a ripe pomegranate on the ground, with a butterfly called a "painted lady" perched on top of it. The painting is signed "Maria Sibylla Gräffin, geb. Merianin. fecit" (Maria Sibylla Graff, born Merian, made this). Though married to Andreas, Maria Sibylla wanted everyone to know that she was a Merian, a member of the renowned family of artists, engravers, and publishers.

In 1668 Andreas and Maria Sibylla moved from Frankfurt to Nuremberg, about 140 miles to the southeast. Like Frankfurt, Nuremberg was a thriving merchant town, and it was also a university town. Andreas had grown up in Nuremberg, where his father was the rector of a school for boys at a Lutheran cathedral. So the move brought Andreas back to his family, but it took Maria Sibylla far away from hers. Though today the trip might only take a couple of hours by train, then it could have taken many days. It was now impossible for Maria Sibylla to see her mother often, though her stepfather did sometimes pass through on his travels.

The Drawing Lesson by Jan Steen, about 1665
While few girls in Maria Sibylla's day were trained to become professional artists, some wealthy women and children came to artists' studios to take drawing lessons as a hobby. In this view of a Dutch studio, there are many props and plaster casts that could be used as models, such as the statue on the table that seems to be the subject of the day's lesson. In Maria Sibylla's studio in Nuremberg, young women were taught to embroider as well as to paint.

Maria Sibylla had her very own garden in Nuremberg, next to the castle church, where she grew flowers and collected insects for her paintings. She spent hours there, sketching insects and writing down her observations about them. On one visit she wrote:

When I went up to my garden to view the flowers and to look for caterpillars, I found a great deal of green slimy deposit on the green leaves of the golden-yellow lilies, so I decided to find out where that slimy deposit came from. Touching it with my little rod, it appeared as if the leaves might be rotting. Then I found in the deposit a great many small, red, round creatures, like small beetles, sitting with their heads very close together and completely immobile, even when I touched them roughly. I then took very many of them home, together with the leaves, in order to investigate what would become of them.

Maria Sibylla was always bringing insects home, along with a supply of the plants they ate. At home it was easier to watch them grow and record their changes from day to day and week to week.

One afternoon, in her kitchen, Maria Sibylla was pleased to find a science experiment taking place right before her eyes. She had been given some birds to cook for dinner. "Three hours later, as I was about to pluck them, there were seventeen fat maggots on them. . . . The next day they changed into completely brown eggs. On August 26th there came out many pretty green and blue flies. I had great difficulty catching these flies, since they were so fast. I got only five of them. All the others escaped." Dinner ruined, Maria Sibylla was still happy to have new insects to observe and write about.

Of course, the family had to make a living, so Maria Sibylla had much to do besides observing insects. There was a new art studio to get up and running. Andreas continued drawing the views of the streets and squares of Nuremberg for which he was best known, and he brought in a printing press to print his engravings. Maria Sibylla carried on with her painting and drawing, not only on vellum but also on silk and linen. She decorated tablecloths with birds and butterflies in paints that would not fade in light or in the laundry. She sold art supplies, including paints that she mixed herself from natural plant and animal sources. And, for the first time, she took in students, all girls from wealthy families. She called them her "company of

Maria Sibylla Merian's Artistic and Scientific Method

Maria Sibylla collected caterpillars and cocoons and brought them home to see what would happen. She took cocoons apart to find out what was inside. She studied the moths and butterflies that emerged from cocoons and watched as the females laid eggs. She saw the eggs hatch into caterpillars. In her study book she made pictures of every stage, arranging them in vertical and horizontal rows.

[1] Maria Sibylla's study of the cream-spot tiger moth began with observing live insects. [2] She made notes and detailed drawings in her study book. [3] She created a design that showed the developmental stages of the tiger moth together with the plant on which it fed as a caterpillar, in this case a hyacinth. The design was engraved and then printed in black ink. [4] The last step was hand-coloring the print using watercolor paints.

[1] Cream-Spot Tiger Moth

[2] **Metamorphosis of the Cream-Spot Tiger Moth** from the study book of Maria Sibylla Merian

[3] **Cream-Spot Tiger Moth and Hyacinth Stalk**, engraving for *The Caterpillar Book* by Maria Sibylla Merian

[4] **Cream-Spot Tiger Moth and Hyacinth Stalk** from *The Caterpillar Book* by Maria Sibylla Merian

From left to right:
Anemone, Fritillary, and Crocus; Crown Imperial; Turk's Cap Lily; and **Bearded Iris** from *The New Book of Flowers* by Maria Sibylla Merian

maidens" and taught them to paint still lifes of flowers like the ones she had learned to make in her stepfather's studio. She also gave embroidery lessons. And perhaps little Johanna took part in the painting and sewing lessons too.

To aid in her teaching, Maria Sibylla decided to produce a book of flowers, "to copy and paint as to sew in the women's room and for the use and pleasure of all expert lovers of art." The flowers in the book would be used as patterns for her students to draw or embroider. She selected blooms that grew from bulbs that were famously popular at the time—tulips, daffodils, irises, and lilies. She also chose plants grown from corms such as pansies and roses. Like her stepfather, she occasionally included butterflies along the margins, where they were less important than the flowers.

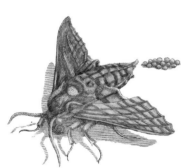

To make her book, she first painted each flower in watercolors on vellum. Then she engraved the lines of the flower onto a copper plate. The plate was put into the printing press to make numerous copies. As a final step, Maria Sibylla carefully colored each print to match the original, using watercolor paints. In 1675 a set of twelve plates was finished, and they were published from the studio of Johann Andreas Graff. The prints were sold together, wrapped in a folder. Maria Sibylla sold some unpainted black-and-white sets. She charged more money for the ones she painted in color. Wealthy buyers could take them to a bookbinder to have them bound in leather, with the title stamped in gold or silver on the cover. But the flower prints were often passed around individually, to be used as patterns. Two more sets of flower prints followed, in 1677 and 1680, and customers could buy them separately, or they could get a new edition that Maria Sibylla prepared with all thirty-six flower pictures. She called this *The New Book of Flowers*.

Seventeenth-Century Science

Microscope by Antonie van Leeuwenhoek, late 1600s

Antonie van Leeuwenhoek invented a microscope with a single glass lens that could magnify an object by more than two hundred times.

Allegory of Geometry by Henri Beaubrun, 1600s

The noblewoman in this painting is Marie-Charlotte de la Trémouille, Duchess of Saxe-Iena. Many people in her day were becoming fascinated with math and science—perhaps this is why she chose to be pictured as the personification of geometry, holding a square ruler and a magnifying glass.

Study of the natural world developed so quickly in the seventeenth century that it has been called a revolution. The change can be summarized as: Don't just accept the wisdom of the past. Question, observe, and come up with new and better explanations. Then challenge those and come up with even better ones.

This attitude was new. For more than fifteen hundred years, ancient Greek and Roman literature and the teachings of the Church had remained the most trusted sources of written information about nature. But around Maria Sibylla's time, people all over Europe started using their own powers of observation and logic to question old ideas and propose new theories. In Italy, Galileo used a new invention—the telescope—to study the stars and planets. He confirmed that the earth moved around the sun, contradicting Aristotle's belief that the sun moved around the earth. In England, William Harvey cut open the veins and arteries of animals to prove that blood was circulated through the body by the pumping heart, not made in the liver, as the Greek doctor Galen had proposed.

Also in England, Isaac Newton observed objects in motion to determine that they fell to earth through the force of gravity. In Holland, Antonie van Leeuwenhoek used a microscope, another new invention, to examine things so small that they had never been seen before, like bacteria and red blood cells. And in Frankfurt, a thirteen-year-old girl with an interest in insects wrote, "All caterpillars, as long as the butterflies have mated beforehand, emerge from their eggs," thus challenging Aristotle's theory of spontaneous generation.

These scientists looked at things differently; they did not accept what others said but set out to discover for themselves. They observed nature closely, and they recorded what they saw. Based on evidence, they developed explanations—hypotheses, or educated guesses—for why things happened the way they did. They were curious, they experimented, and they shared their ideas so that others might build on them. Today we call their approach the scientific method.

Magnifying Glass, about 1700

The practice of grinding glass on a curve to enable it to magnify had been known for centuries, but in Maria Sibylla's time the process was highly refined. In Amsterdam, jewelers looked through magnifying lenses when they cut diamonds. Scientists were beginning to use magnification too, to see details in specimens from the natural world that could not be observed with the naked eye. Maria Sibylla used magnifying lenses to examine tiny insect eggs and hard-to-see body parts of ants, spiders, and caterpillars.

Beehive in a Floral Wreath from *The Caterpillar Book* by Maria Sibylla Merian

For the first image in the second volume of *The Caterpillar Book*, Maria Sibylla chose to illustrate the honeybee. She had placed the silkworm at the beginning of the first volume, and once again she highlighted an insect that is useful to humans.

Maria Sibylla gave birth to a second daughter, Dorothea, in 1678. She also began another book, *Caterpillars, Their Wondrous Transformation and Peculiar Nourishment from Flowers*, published in 1679. Based on Maria Sibylla's years of observation, note taking, and sketching, this was a scientific book "wherein by means of an entirely new invention the origin, food, and development of caterpillars, worms, butterflies, moths, flies, and other such little animals, including times, places, and characteristics . . . are diligently examined, briefly described, painted from nature, engraved in copper, and published independently." The "new invention" Maria Sibylla mentioned, "a so-called magnifying glass," could be used "to discover things that could not be seen with the naked eye." Though magnifying glasses had been invented much earlier, Maria Sibylla might have been referring to a new type of lens that was stronger than those available in the past.

In this book, often simply called *The Caterpillar Book*, Maria Sibylla put the caterpillars at center stage and gave the flowers supporting roles. Based on the

Sweet Violet with Honeybee
from *The Caterpillar Book* by Maria Sibylla Merian

Maria Sibylla starts her illustration of the life cycle of the honeybee with the caterpillar. The pupal stage has six feet. The next stage, she explained, turns brown and has a sting. The three stages of the life cycle are seen at the bottom of the picture, and at the top is the fully developed bee with extended wings. On the left Maria Sibylla included the metamorphosis of the wax moth, an enemy of the honeybee.

drawings in her study book, she created pictures showing the metamorphosis of each caterpillar, and she also showed the plant on which the caterpillar fed. Then, for each picture, she wrote a description from her notes, telling the reader what she had observed. Maria Sibylla pointed out, for example, that some insects ate only one kind of plant and would die if their special food was not available. Others adapted to eating something else but would return to their favorite food when they could find it. Some insects liked to eat other insects and might even eat their own offspring.

Maria Sibylla prepared the plates of *The Caterpillar Book* just as she had done for the flower books, but this time there were fifty plates to get ready all at once, instead of just twelve, and written descriptions to be set into type. The first plate in the book pictured the metamorphosis of the silkworm (see page 17).

The Caterpillar Book showed that Maria Sibylla Merian was not just an artist who painted caterpillars but a scientist who could explain their life cycles. Each stage of an insect's metamorphosis, from egg to caterpillar to pupa to moth or

Red Currant with Peppered Moth
from *The Caterpillar Book* by Maria Sibylla Merian

Brown Lappet Moth from *The Caterpillar Book* by Maria Sibylla Merian

The brown lappet is one of the largest moths, and its caterpillars can change color according to the plant they live on. When Maria Sibylla reared some of the different-colored caterpillars, they all metamorphosed into the same type of pupa and adult. With this drawing of one brown and one black-and-white caterpillar, she made one of the first scientific observations of camouflage in insects.

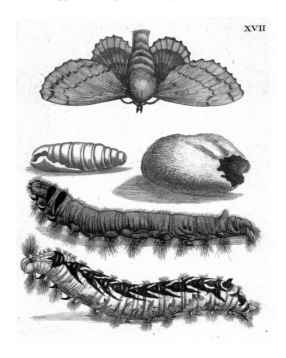

Predators, Parasites, and Parasitoids

Because Maria Sibylla studied insects in nature, she knew their enemies. In her picture of a honeybee on the opposite page, she also showed the wax moth larva, which feeds on beeswax and can destroy a hive. With the pineapple on page 53, she shows a ladybug—a predator that kills and feeds on other insects—along with its prey, the cochineal beetle (which happens to be used to make carmine red pigment). Predatory spiders and ants are pictured on page 61. Maria Sibylla was one of the first to record observations of predatory behavior in insects.

In other paintings, Maria Sibylla shows parasites, which live on host organisms without killing them, and parasitoids, which live on their hosts and kill them. One of Maria Sibylla's contributions to biology was her early observation of parasitoids. At first she was confused by what she called "false and useless metamorphoses," when, for example, a fly would emerge from a cocoon instead of the butterfly she was expecting. After observing this phenomenon among many different species, she came to recognize parasitoids in nature.

In drawings [2–4] on page 27, there are winged insects on the lower right. These are ichneumon wasps, parasitoids of the cream-spot tiger moth. The female ichneumon wasp deposits its eggs in or around a caterpillar. After the caterpillar spins its cocoon, the wasp eggs hatch into tiny larvae that feed on the host caterpillar. Then they undergo metamorphosis from larvae to pupae to adult wasps and emerge from the cocoon. Maria Sibylla's drawing depicts both the adult tiger moth and also the parasitoid that sometimes emerged in its place. Though she might have been disappointed when she

first saw these "midgets" come out from the cocoons she had been watching, she was a true scientist and recorded everything she observed.

In her drawing of the life cycle of the antler moth (right), Maria Sibylla shows a tachinid fly parasitoid. The green-and-white caterpillar is that of the antler moth. The fly lays its eggs on the caterpillar, and after the caterpillar spins its cocoon, tachinid larvae hatch and feed on the caterpillar. Then they complete their metamorphosis into adult flies. Maria Sibylla shows the fly on the left and a broken pupa from which a tachinid fly has emerged.

Ichneumon Wasp from *The Caterpillar Book* by Maria Sibylla Merian

Wild Larkspur, Antler Moth, and Tachinid Fly from *The Caterpillar Book* by Maria Sibylla Merian

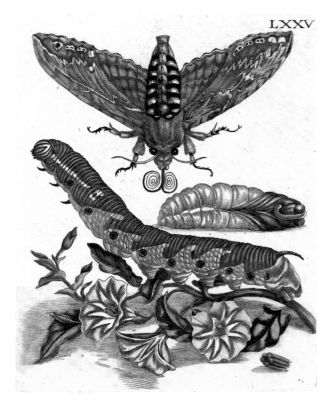

Sloe Plant with Eggar Moth from *The Caterpillar Book* by Maria Sibylla Merian

Maria Sibylla found this large cocoon containing more than seventy small caterpillars. She referred to it as a "sun nest," since it was built on the sunny side of the plant to get maximum warmth. These silken webs control the temperature and act like greenhouses for the caterpillars, which can enter and exit through a small opening. Maria Sibylla observed that when the sun came out, all the caterpillars entered their "apartment" and remained there until the heat had passed. These caterpillars of the eggar moth live together in social groups until halfway through the final larval stage.

Bindweed with Convolvulus Hawk Moth from *The Caterpillar Book* by Maria Sibylla Merian

This moth's unusually long proboscis enables it to feed on the nectar of long, tubular flowers, like those of the bindweed plant. The coloring of the caterpillar helps it hide among the flowers and leaves.

butterfly, was shown life size. The insects were so perfectly painted that they looked like photographs—except that of course photography would not be invented for more than a century. Males were distinguished from females, and the plants and flowers that were the caterpillars' food and habitat were pictured accurately, though not always life size.

These were three innovations by Maria Sibylla: showing insects in all the stages of their lives in a single painting, linking insects to the plants on which they fed, and including written descriptions. *The Caterpillar Book* made Maria Sibylla one of the world's first entomologists and ecologists, long before those words had been invented.

In 1682 there was a dramatic change in Maria Sibylla's life. The year after her stepfather died, she and her daughters left Nuremberg and returned to Frankfurt to live with her widowed mother. Her mother helped care for Johanna and Dorothea, and Maria Sibylla continued to study and paint local insects. Andreas was with her and the girls in Frankfurt for at least some of the time, and he helped publish the second volume of *The Caterpillar Book* in 1683. But in the summer of 1685 he returned to Nuremberg alone. It was a sign that the marriage might not have been as happy as everyone had hoped.

LXXXVIII

Field Eryngo Thistle with Map-Winged Butterfly, Ichneumon Wasp, and Lesser Pearl Butterfly from *The Caterpillar Book* by Maria Sibylla Merian

Chapter three
Transforming Her Life

"Maria Sibylla Merian made this."

    Maria Sibylla Merian

It was a radical step for Maria Sibylla to take. Without her husband, she moved with her mother and daughters to a new country—Holland. Her older half brother Caspar Merian now lived there in a religious community led by Jean de Labadie, a Jesuit priest who became a Calvinist and was convinced that to live a godly life, one had to separate from the world. He and his followers had been driven out of one town after another until a supporter offered them Waltha Castle in Wieuwerd, in a region of northwest Holland called Friesland. There, several hundred people lived together under strict religious discipline. They studied the Bible and prayed throughout the day. They ate simple food, wore coarse clothing, and forbade adornments such as lace or jewelry. Each person had to contribute; in 1685, when Maria Sibylla moved in, she gave the Labadists one-quarter of her wealth. And everyone had a job to do—in the garden, the laundry, the bakery—because the community was self-sufficient.

Johanna was seventeen and Dorothea only seven when they joined the Labadists. It was a completely new way of life, and not an easy one. The change must have been difficult for them. Andreas visited Wieuwerd at least twice. But in 1690 he and Maria Sibylla divorced, at a time when divorce was a great scandal.

Caspar died in 1686, but Maria Sibylla and her mother and daughters stayed at Wieuwerd. They kept busy with their chores in the community, and Maria Sibylla continued her scientific studies. Johanna and Dorothea learned to draw and to paint using watercolors. And just like their mother, they developed their skills of observation and came to look at the world through artists' eyes.

Sweet Cherry with Emperor Moth and Tortricid Moth from *The Caterpillar Book* by Maria Sibylla Merian

Waltha Castle by Johann Andreas Graff, 1686–90

Andreas visited Maria Sibylla and their daughters at Waltha Castle, perhaps hoping to reunite his family. He stayed long enough to draw several images of the estate where the Labadists established a community.

Maria Sibylla was making sketches and notes for a third volume of *The Caterpillar Book*. She also began to study bats and frogs. She wrote in her study book:

In April the frogs laid a large quantity of little eggs. I cut open the female and found in her a womb like all other animals have. They do not give birth through their mouths, as many writers have thought. In the womb I found a quantity of such seeds as were seen in the female. In early May I took some of the frog eggs I had found in a frog's dead body at the water's edge. I dug up some young grass with earth and put it into a bowl. I poured water on it, and threw in bread. I did this every day. After several days the little black specks began to show life and fed on the white slime that surrounded them. Later they grew little tails so that they could swim in the water like fish. In the middle of May they developed eyes. Eight days later two little feet broke through the skin. After eight more days another two little feet broke through the skin towards the front. They looked like little crocodiles. Then the tail rotted away. They were real frogs and jumped onto land.

Metamorphosis of a Frog by Maria Sibylla
Merian, 1701–5

While at Waltha Castle, Maria Sibylla became
interested in frogs. She captured them, studied
them, and drew the various stages in their
development—from eggs to tadpoles to full-
grown frogs. Maria Sibylla was one of the first
to record this transformation, at a time when
scientists were still debating how frogs man-
aged to live both on land and in water.

Barbastelle Bat with Orb Weaver Spider by
Maria Sibylla Merian, 1691–99

Most bats use echolocation to find their prey—
they send out sound waves and listen for the
echoes that bounce back from insects as well
as other objects. Certain moths with ears can
detect the sound waves and avoid being eaten.
The barbastelle is known as the "whispering
bat" because the sound waves it emits are so
quiet, it can sneak up even on hearing moths.
Maria Sibylla may have added an orb weaver
spider to her drawing because spiders are also
common prey for bats.

Amsterdam City View by Jan van der Heyden, about 1670

In moving to Amsterdam, Maria Sibylla chose to live
and work in one of the most important cities in Europe.
It was the capital of a far-flung Dutch empire that had
trading posts and colonies in the Americas, the Persian
Gulf, India, and the East Indies. Dutch ships carried goods
throughout the world, and Amsterdam's merchants made
fortunes buying and selling spices and sugar, tulips and
tobacco, Turkish carpets and Chinese porcelain, and just
about anything that a wealthy seventeenth-century person
would want to buy. The city was also a center of banking
and finance, ship building, and diamond cutting.

This painting depicts houses on the Herengracht, one of
three semicircular canals that drain and manage water for
this low-lying city, built on marshy ground near the edge
of the North Sea. The canals also served as transportation
networks, carrying barge traffic in the warm months and
ice skaters in the winter.

The Labadists sent missionaries to the Dutch colony of Surinam, in South
America, to establish another community and to convert native peoples to their
religious views. While she was at Waltha Castle, Maria Sibylla saw preserved
animals that the missionaries had sent back to Wieuwerd from Surinam. She
was fascinated, having never seen creatures like these before.

Six years after joining the Labadists, Maria Sibylla and her daughters left the
community. There could have been many reasons, including the death of Maria
Sibylla's mother the year before. In 1691, Johanna, Dorothea, and Maria Sibylla
moved to Amsterdam and changed their lives again.

Women Artists in Northern Europe

Self-Portrait by Judith Leyster, about 1630

Lace Model Book by Rosina Helena Fürst, about 1660

It was unusual for a woman to become a professional artist during the seventeenth century. In Germany and Holland, most women were busy keeping house, raising children, and supporting family businesses, and opportunities for training or careers outside the home were almost nonexistent. The few women who did become professional artists were often daughters in artistic families who, like Maria Sibylla, were trained by their fathers, brothers, or other relatives.

Rosina Helena Fürst, born in 1642 and just five years older than Maria Sibylla, grew up in Nuremberg in a family of engravers and printers, and she became a designer of patterns for lace and embroidery. She wrote, "The Lord God did not ordain that only male persons should work. He also gave females eyes with which to see, ears with which to hear, and a tongue with which to speak. He filled their hearts with understanding. He also gave them hands with which to work, not to be laid in their laps but used to honest purpose and to create something good."

The painter and printmaker Geertruydt Roghman, born in Amsterdam in 1625, was the daughter and granddaughter of artists. One of her engravings of women at work appears on page 18.

There were a few women born into wealthy families who could afford private lessons and had the freedom to pursue artistic careers. Judith Leyster, a Dutch artist who lived a little earlier than Maria Sibylla, belonged to a family that made beer. She was allowed to take lessons and became a successful painter of portraits and scenes of everyday life. She joined a painters' guild—one of two women of her time admitted to membership in this type of professional association.

The artist Rachel Ruysch was the daughter of Frederik Ruysch, a professor of anatomy who was a friend of Maria Sibylla's in Amsterdam. Rachel painted still lifes, and she might have been inspired by Maria Sibylla to include insects and other small animals in her paintings. But she was less concerned with portraying nature accurately and showed combinations of animals, fruits, and flowers that would not normally be found together. Still, her paintings were very beautiful and extremely popular.

These and other women artists, including Maria Sibylla, are now recognized for their pioneering roles in the art of northern Europe.

Still Life with Fruit and Insects by Rachel Ruysch, 1711

Pear Branch with Blue-Backed Manakin
by Maria Sibylla Merian and Johanna Herolt?,
1693–99

Mice with Acorns and Nuts by Maria Sibylla
Merian and Johanna Herolt?, 1691–99

In Amsterdam, Maria Sibylla's daughters helped
her to produce artworks, and it is now hard to tell
who painted which pictures. Both Maria Sibylla and
Johanna painted similar versions of pear branches
and mice.

Amsterdam was nothing like Wieuwerd, or even Nuremberg or Frankfurt. It was
the third largest city in Europe, and also a center of art, science, and publishing. Here
lived painters and printers, mapmakers and engravers, scientists and lovers of nature,
and—important to Maria Sibylla—people who could afford to buy art. In Amsterdam, women had the legal right to own property and run businesses. It was a
place where Maria Sibylla and her daughters hoped they could find happiness
and success.

Together, they set up a studio and began to paint. Sometimes they
traced images from the printed sheets of Maria Sibylla's previous books
and hand-colored them for sale. They made new prints from the

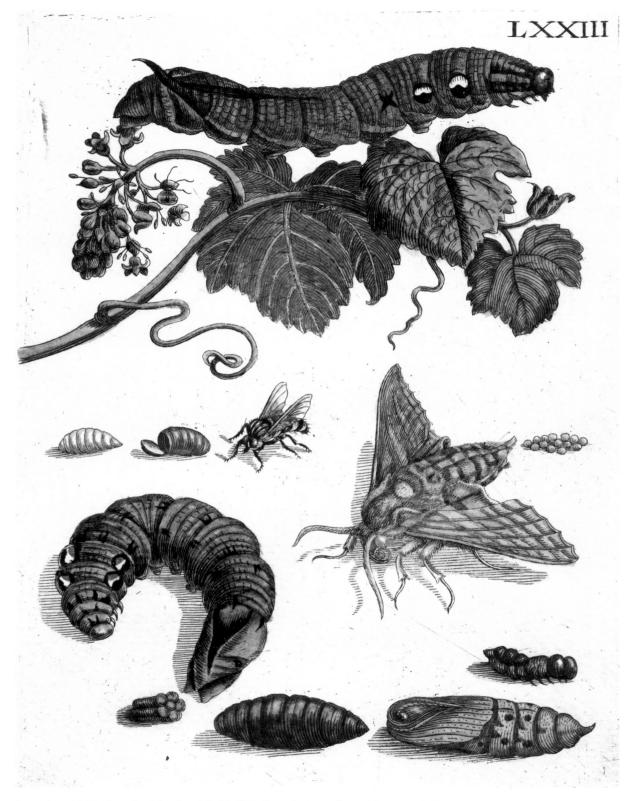

Grapevine with Elephant Hawk Moth and Tachinid Fly from *The Caterpillar Book* by Maria Sibylla Merian

Late Spring Flowers in a Glass Vase with Self-Portrait by Johanna Herolt, 1695–98

In Amsterdam, Johanna began to paint independently of her mother, and she specialized in still-life watercolors of flowers. On the glass vase in this picture she painted her own reflection. Johanna portrayed herself wearing the plain black dress of a Labadist woman, with her hair hidden under a black cap that comes to a point on her forehead.

copper plates Maria Sibylla had brought with her to Amsterdam. They also created entirely new drawings of plants and flowers and birds and insects. To speed things up, Johanna and Dorothea occasionally finished paintings started by their mother, but Maria Sibylla always signed them. Her signature now said, simply, "Maria Sibylla Merian fec"—"Maria Sibylla Merian made this."

Johanna began to paint on her own, sometimes copying her mother's drawings but signing them herself, and also designing her own paintings. She hoped to become an independent artist like her mother one day. In 1692 she married Jacob Hendrik Herolt, a merchant who had also once lived with the Labadists.

By now Merian drawings were known for their accuracy, and they were sought after by collectors and naturalists. It seems that in Amsterdam—where the microscope had been invented—Maria Sibylla and her daughters had access to stronger magnifying glasses than they had used before. Now they were able to paint tiny details with even greater precision—a bristle on a caterpillar's back, for example, and the "veins" in the transparent wing of a wasp—using a single hair of a paintbrush.

Not even the smallest ant escaped Maria Sibylla's close attention. "On 25 July 1694," she wrote, "I found a whole nest of ants, large and small, with and without wings, many thousands. I have painted four of them here." These drawings would become the basis for the first plate in the third volume of *The Caterpillar Book*.

For painters of flowers and fruits, Amsterdam was a paradise. The city's Hortus Medicus, once a garden of herbs used in medicines, now displayed exotic plants from all over the world. On its garden paths Maria Sibylla and her daughters could see

Ants in a Floral Wreath from *The Caterpillar Book* by Maria Sibylla Merian

Apricot Branch with Leaf-Roller Moth from *The Caterpillar Book* by Maria Sibylla Merian

Maria Sibylla worked on the third volume of *The Caterpillar Book* throughout the 1690s. The caterpillar here is one that she first collected at Waltha Castle. "I have often found these attractive yellow and black speckled caterpillars on apricots, cherries, and damsons," she wrote. "One spun a cocoon in Wieuwerd in August 1690, and in June of the following year a grayish moth emerged. . . . I found similar caterpillars in Amsterdam that duly proceeded to spin cocoons," she continued. "This metamorphosis can be seen in my third caterpillar book." This insect is called a leaf-roller moth because the caterpillar rolls itself into the leaf it feeds on, spins a silken covering, and pupates within the leaf roll. Maria Sibylla wrote that from one of the cocoons emerged a small caterpillar that metamorphosed into "a black fly." It was actually a wasp that is a parasitoid of the leaf-roller moth.

Honeysuckle with Privet Hawk Moth and Tachinid Fly from *The Caterpillar Book* by Maria Sibylla Merian

When disturbed, the male privet hawk moth makes a hissing sound by rubbing scales over spines at the end of the abdomen. Maria Sibylla collected a number of the green caterpillars but reported that many of them died, and that flies emerged from the dead caterpillars. The flies are parasitoids, which consume their hosts.

carefully cultivated tropical plants that were entirely new to the people of Europe. In the winter these were brought into greenhouses so they would not freeze. In another building, visitors could examine butterflies pinned in cases and tropical birds and animals that were stuffed or preserved in jars.

Maria Sibylla and her daughters also visited a garden owned by Agnes Block, where fruit trees bloomed and colorful birds were housed in aviaries. Block was also an artist, and she delighted in exchanging seeds and plants with other collectors throughout Europe and then inviting local artists to come and paint them.

Maria Sibylla's interest in nature drew her into a circle of collectors who traded in exotic animal specimens, most of which were gathered by Dutch merchants and

seamen during their travels. Some collectors were scholars, but many were wealthy individuals with an intense curiosity about the natural world. They showcased their collections in what they called curiosity cabinets, or rooms of wonder, where rare shells, gemstones, and dried plants were displayed on shelves, colorful butterflies and beetles were pinned onto boards, small animals were preserved in jars with alcohol, and stuffed birds or even a crocodile might hang from the ceiling.

Corresponding by mail with collectors across Europe, Maria Sibylla sold and exchanged rare animal and plant specimens. She had engaged in this trade in a small way in Nuremberg, but in Amsterdam she expanded her activities. In 1697 she wrote to a friend in Nuremberg, "There are many rarities from the East and West Indies to be had here in Holland as well. If anyone is a collector, I shall be happy to send some," adding "and if anyone desires any kind of seeds from plants abundant in the Indies, they may be obtained here too." The buying and selling of preserved specimens increased Maria Sibylla's income, adding to what she and her daughters earned from their paintings.

TAB. I.

Fig. II.

Cabinet of Curiosities by Ferrante Imperato, 1599

Preserved Animal Specimens by Frederik Ruysch, about 1725

Maria Sibylla was one of many Europeans fascinated by the natural world. Long-distance trade with India and China and explorations of the Americas made it possible for Europeans to see plants, animals, shells, and minerals they had never heard of before, and they began to collect and display them in what they called rooms of wonder. In Naples, Ferrante Imperato wrote a book cataloguing his collection of shells, birds, fossils, gems, minerals, and even a prized crocodile. In Amsterdam, Maria Sibylla's friend Frederik Ruysch preserved animal specimens in his own secret blend of alcohol. Collectors corresponded with each other, exchanging and selling rare specimens and even traveling to distant lands to see them. These rooms of wonder preceded the great natural history museums of later eras.

Some of the animal specimens that interested Maria Sibylla the most were from Surinam, the Dutch colony on the northeast coast of South America where the Labadists had established a mission. She began to collect the samples, perhaps with the help of Johanna's husband, a merchant who traded in Surinam. Maria Sibylla also had her own contacts there, "who catch such animals and send them to me," she wrote. So she was familiar with the tropical beetles and butterflies that were prized by collectors, but unhappy that the ones she saw were dried and lifeless, drained of their natural color, and separated from their habitats. Europeans knew almost nothing about them—not where they lived, what they ate, or the cycles of their metamorphosis. "In Holland," she later wrote, "I was astounded to see what lovely creatures were brought back from the East and West Indies . . . but their origin and manner of reproduction were lacking, that is, how they transform themselves from caterpillars into butterflies and so forth. All this inspired me to undertake a long and costly journey, and to sail to Surinam in America . . . to pursue my observations." Maria Sibylla made the bold decision to travel across the ocean to the jungles of Surinam to see the insects for herself, so she could study them and paint them from life in their natural habitats.

But how would she pay for such a journey? In February 1699 this advertisement appeared in the *Amsterdam Current* newspaper:

An excellent, aesthetically pleasing and curious body of work by Maria Sibylla Merian, consisting of rare herbs, flowers, fruits, and the observation of bloodless animals, each on its food, all painted in water-color (from nature, with exceptionally beautiful colors on parchment in folio); also East and West Indian plants and animals, including descriptions of the above, gathered at great expense and with great effort over a period of 30 years in Germany, Holland and Friesland, consisting of 253 sheets and 2 other works of smaller format, a Hortus Eystattensis *complete, annotated, and colored, and 100 etched copper Plates.*

Maria Sibylla sold her artwork and collections to pay for the trip. It would be dangerous, so before she left, she wrote her will. Then she packed sea chests with paints and vellum, magnifying glasses, wooden boxes, and specimen jars. She would take Dorothea along to help her, but Johanna would stay behind with her husband in Amsterdam, where she would continue to paint. In June 1699 Maria Sibylla and Dorothea boarded a merchant ship bound for Surinam.

Chapter four
Danger, Discovery, Adventure

"I almost had to pay for it with my life."

      Maria Sibylla Merian

As soon as they set foot on the ship, Maria Sibylla, now fifty-two, and Dorothea, twenty-one, became world travelers embarking on a scientific expedition. The sea voyage was thrilling at first, with the chance of spotting turtles, whales, dolphins, and flying fish during the day, and vast nighttime skies filled with stars. But there were also plundering pirates and ship-wrecking hurricanes to worry about, and the choppy waters of the Atlantic made everyone seasick. The lodgings on the ship were neither comfortable nor private. To sleep, Maria Sibylla and Dorothea, along with the other passengers, who were mostly men, descended below deck to a dank, smelly area crowded with narrow bunks. During storms, if they could sleep at all, they might

Citron with Harlequin Long-Horned Beetle and Monkey Slug Moth from *The Insects of Surinam* by Maria Sibylla Merian

Shipping in a Calm by Jan van de Cappelle, 1649

In the mid-1600s the Dutch Republic was at the height of its power as a global trading empire, and its sailing vessels were among the best in the world. Its battleships and cargo carriers dominated the seas and crowded into busy ports, like this one at Vlissingen. Maria Sibylla and Dorothea most likely sailed on a square-rigged fluyt, a ship about eighty feet long, designed to transport cargo rather than passengers.

Pineapple and Cockroaches from *The Insects of Surinam* by Maria Sibylla Merian

Pineapple and Scarce Bamboo Page Butterfly from *The Insects of Surinam* by Maria Sibylla Merian

"Since the pineapple is the most important of all edible fruits, it is only right that it is also the first of this work and of my findings," Maria Sibylla wrote in the first entry of *The Insects of Surinam*. She did not give any reason for the pineapple's importance, other than the fact that she liked to eat it. In contrast to her favorite fruit, she shows one of the insects she liked the least. "Cockroaches are the most notorious of all insects in America," she wrote, "due to the great damage and inconveniences they cause to all inhabitants, spoiling all their wool, linen, food, and drink." Maria Sibylla shows two types of cockroaches and describes their metamorphosis, which is very different from that of butterflies and moths. A cockroach hatches looking similar to an adult, except for its undeveloped wings and genitalia. After molting five to seven times, the adult winged cockroach emerges.

In the second image, along with the golden ripe pineapple, Maria Sibylla shows a scarce bamboo page butterfly and a ladybug. She notes that the larvae of the ladybug is a predator of the cochineal—the insect used to make carmine red pigment. Her description is one of the first notations of predatory behavior by insects.

awaken with water dripping on their heads from cracks in the deck above them. Some passengers slept in the same clothes for the entire journey. There were no bathrooms, only chamber pots that had to be emptied over the side of the ship. The food was always the same—cabbage, potatoes, and salted meat and fish. After two months at sea, mother and daughter longed for steady earth under their feet and fresh food to eat.

How happy they were to reach Surinam, where guavas, papayas, oranges, bananas, and other fruit grew within easy reach. Maria Sibylla tasted pineapple for the first time, and she described it as a combination of grapes, apricots, currants, apples, and pears, with a fragrance that could fill a room. She chose two drawings of pineapples to be the first pictures in a new book she was already planning—*The Insects of Surinam.*

The sights and sounds of South America were strange to Maria Sibylla and Dorothea; the tropics were nothing like the European countryside they knew. Trees soared more than a hundred feet overhead. Monkeys chattered and cicadas buzzed. Large birds in outlandish colors strutted by on long legs. Huge butterflies flashed bright blue iridescent wings. Maria Sibylla couldn't wait to begin exploring, to see what new insects and plants she would find in this place she had dreamed of visiting for so long.

Guava with Tiger Wing Butterfly and Flannel Moth from *The Insects of Surinam* by Maria Sibylla Merian

Maria Sibylla found the guava fruit "pleasant to eat, both raw as well as cooked." She was fascinated by the fat striped caterpillars she found on the guava trees, with their shiny red beads and black hairs. She wrote about them to the microscopist Antonie van Leeuwenhoek, who thought the beads might be eyes. But Maria Sibylla wasn't convinced. In her view, if they were eyes, then the caterpillars "should be able to discover their food from behind and from the side, which I have so far not been able to establish." Her observations always included insect behavior as well as appearance.

But first the women had to get settled. They moved into a house with a small garden in Paramaribo, the colony's capital. There a few hundred people, mostly from Holland, Germany, and England, lived in European-style wooden homes. Maria Sibylla and Dorothea were probably the only European women living there without a male relative. Most of the residents were businessmen, soldiers, sailors, agents of the Dutch West India Company, and plantation owners. Few were interested in the insects and plants that had lured Maria Sibylla to the continent. She wrote that "the people there have no desire to investigate such things; indeed they mocked me for seeking something other than sugar in that country."

Maria Sibylla didn't even have to leave the house to find new and interesting creatures. A blue lizard laid eggs in the corner of a room. Cockroaches that ventured inside

Scarlet Ibis by Maria Sibylla Merian or
Dorothea Graff, 1699–1700

The scarlet ibis—labeled here as the Surinam
flamingo—is native to the wetlands and marshes
along the northeastern coast of South America
and the Caribbean islands. It is possible that
this picture was actually painted by Dorothea,
as it shows the bird and its egg but not its natural habitat. Maria Sibylla normally included
plants in her paintings of animals.

were captured for study. The garden received visits from hummingbirds and butterflies, and it was full of beetles and all sorts of caterpillars. She quickly discovered
that the insects of the tropics could be more dangerous than those at home—when
she touched one hairy white caterpillar, her hand swelled up painfully.

Maria Sibylla used her magnifying glass to see and paint tiny insect eggs and
to inspect new specimens. Examining some moths, she remarked, "As beautiful as
they are when observed without the magnifying glass, they are weirdly bristly and
ugly when seen through it."

Surinam

Surinam (also spelled Suriname) is a small
country that sits just above the equator on
the northeast coast of South America. Hot,
humid, and thick with rivers, it encompasses
mountains, tropical grasslands, and rain
forests so dense they still have not been fully
explored. Its first inhabitants were indigenous
groups, including Carib, Arawak, and other
smaller tribes.

In the seventeenth century English colonists established plantations in Surinam.
They offered a degree of religious tolerance to
Jewish settlers who came there from Portugal,
Holland, and nearby Brazil. The Dutch also
set up plantations there, and during a war
with England, Dutch warships seized the
colony. The Treaty of Breda that ended the
war declared that the Dutch would keep

**Slave Gathering
on a Sugar Plan-
tation in Surinam**
by Dirk Valkenburg,
1706–8

Surinam, with its profitable sugar plantations and
rich natural resources, but the English could have
the North American colony of New Amsterdam,
which they renamed New York.

In Maria Sibylla's time Surinam was a Dutch
colony. From 1683 to 1688 its governor was Cor-
nelis van Aerssen van Sommelsdijck, the owner of
Waltha Castle, where Maria Sibylla had lived with
the Labadists. Some Labadists owned plantations
along the coast and the rivers, where the land
was flat and fertile, and those are the ones Maria
Sibylla and Dorothea visited.

Planters in Surinam grew primarily sugar,
but also coffee, cocoa, and cotton.
To work their plantations they
brought slaves from Africa.
They also tried to enslave
the native Caribs and
Arawaks. Maria Sibylla
referred to the native people as "Indians" and "slaves."
Slavery was always brutal, but on
the sugar plantations of Surinam it
was especially harsh.

Sugar was not native to the
Americas but was introduced by

Map of the West Indies from *The Sea Atlas* by John Seller, 1675

Maria Sibylla and Dorothea visited sugar plantations along the rivers of Surinam to see what insects and plants they might discover there. They were shocked by the number of enslaved Africans and native Amerindians they saw working under harsh conditions. Maria Sibylla disapproved of how the European planters treated slaves, and she expressed this attitude when writing about a plant the native women used to avoid having children:

The seeds of this plant (called the "peacock flower") are used by women who have labor pains in order to hasten the birth. The Indians (who are not well-treated by the Dutch), use the seeds so they will not produce children, so that their children will not become slaves like they are. The black slaves from Guinea and Angola have demanded to be treated well. Otherwise they refuse to have children. In fact, they commit suicide because they are treated so badly. They believe that they will be born again, free and living in their own land. They told me this themselves.

Maria Sibylla employed African slaves and also native men and women. She needed help, and it did not occur to her to challenge the inhumane institution of slavery. She did write that slaves "must be treated kindly."

Europeans as a cash crop. Slaves cleared the land, planted and cut the sugarcane, and processed it in sugar mills before it was shipped to Europe. Previously, Europeans had only honey to sweeten their food, but once sugar became widely available, they could not get enough of it.

This love for sweetness spread only because the enslavement of Africans made it possible. In Surinam, many Africans escaped into the tropical forests with the help of local Indians. They established their own communities and were known as Maroons. Maria Sibylla did not approve of the treatment the slaves received from owners and overseers, nor did she think it wise for the colony's economy to be so dependent on the cultivation of sugar. Of all the plants that grew in the tropics, she never drew sugarcane, or the insects that fed on it.

Plantation in Surinam by Caspar Barlaeus, 1647

This engraving shows slaves transporting what is probably sugar from a plantation in the distance. Two balance heavy sacks on their heads, while a European overseer rides along on horseback. The rugged terrain forces the group to travel along the shallow river, with their feet and the wheels of the cart sinking into the mud.

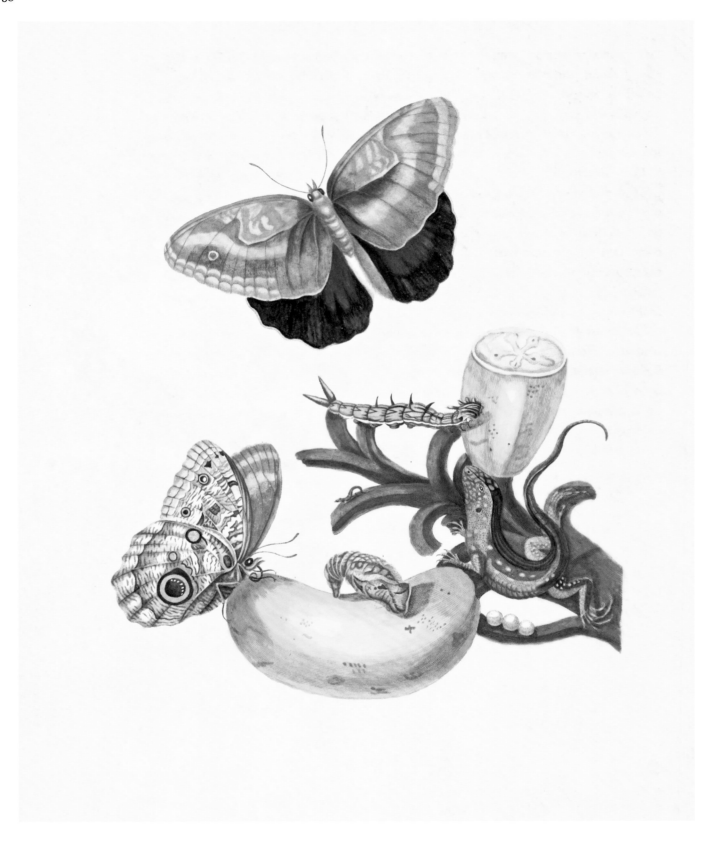

Banana with Teucer Giant Owl Butterfly and Rainbow Whiptail Lizard from *The Insects of Surinam* by Maria Sibylla Merian

This rainbow whiptail lizard made its nest in Maria Sibylla's house. Her drawing not only introduced European readers to this unusual creature, it also shows a tropical fruit they had probably never seen before—a banana. In the jungles of Surinam bananas grew abundantly, but there was no way to transport them to Europe before they spoiled. Maria Sibylla shows four stages of the Teucer giant owl butterfly: eggs, a brown caterpillar with an unusual arrow-shaped head, a wood-colored chrysalis, and an adult with brilliant blue hind wings.

Peacock Flower and Tobacco Hornworm from *The Insects of Surinam* by Maria Sibylla Merian

Some children in Surinam kept the brightly colored tobacco hornworm as a pet. The peacock flower was a popular plant in the gardens of Paramaribo and could grow as high as nine feet. Native women grew the plant for its medicinal properties. They told Maria Sibylla that they used it to keep from having children, because they didn't want their sons or daughters to be slaves.

The native women helped Maria Sibylla with housekeeping and showed her how things were done in the tropics. They spun cotton to make the hammocks in which they slept and laid bread on banana leaves to bake. They were especially helpful in Maria Sibylla's study of plants, because they had women's traditional knowledge about how to use herbs and wild plants as medicines, and they knew which species could be eaten and which were poisonous. They pointed out the gummi guttae tree, which yielded a resin similar to gum arabic that could be used as a binder for watercolors. And they taught Maria Sibylla how to make a black dye and a bright red dye from the seeds of the rocu tree. The native people used these colors to paint decorative patterns on their skin.

Rocu Tree with Fire-Tip Skipper Butterfly and Sweet Potato Armyworm Moth from *The Insects of Surinam* by Maria Sibylla Merian

Maria Sibylla wrote that the rocu tree produces "lovely red seeds. The Indians put these in water to soften. Then the red dye comes off and sinks to the bottom. Afterwards they gradually pour off the water and dry the dye that lies at the bottom. With it they paint all sorts of figures on their naked skin, which constitute their adornment."

Spiders, Ants, and an Ecosystem

In a single picture Maria Sibylla shows biodiversity in the jungles of South America. Here she portrays a variety of living things—spiders, ants, a hummingbird, a cockroach—preying on each other or being preyed upon. The impression is very different from Maria Sibylla's earliest drawings of lovely flowers with butterflies in all their stages of development. This image shows a dangerous habitat where organisms eat or are eaten.

The brown spider in the upper right is an orb weaver, with new young spiders emerging from its egg sac on a circular web. Maria Sibylla wrote, "The spider shown here on its web carries its eggs on a sac under its body, where they hatch." On the top left is a huntsman spider, and both spider webs at the top are shown with army ants, which the spiders feed on. Maria Sibylla was amazed at the ability of army ants to link together to form a bridge. She wrote, "The first ant sits still and bites into a piece of wood, the second places itself behind the first and clings tightly to it, similarly the third, and so on. And then they let the wind blow them until they have reached the other side." On a branch of the guava tree below, ants are attacking a cockroach.

Maria Sibylla explained how leaf-cutter ants sliced leaves with their mandibles, which she described as "two hooked teeth which slide along each other like scissors." These ants, she said, "can make whole trees go bald as brooms in a single night so the tree looks like the trees in Europe in winter." Maria Sibylla thought the ants took cut leaves to the nest to feed their young. In fact, leaf-cutter ants use the leaves to cultivate fungus as food for themselves and their larvae. Maria Sibylla was the first scientist to describe army ants and leaf-cutter ants.

The two largest spiders in the picture are tarantulas. They are known to eat birds, bats, rats, frogs, insects, lizards, and small snakes. They live in burrows, which the females line with silk. On the left, Maria Sibylla shows one tarantula with a silk burrow guarding its egg sac while feeding on an ant it has captured in its fangs. These fangs also bite and inject paralyzing venom, allowing the spider to suck juices from its prey. That is what the spider on the right is doing to the hummingbird. Maria Sibylla wrote in her study book, "If there is a lack of ants they drag little birds from their nests and suck all the blood from the body." This particular hummingbird does not match any known species, and scientists think it may now be extinct.

For many years Europeans thought this drawing was inaccurate, because they could not imagine a spider eating a bird. But when the British naturalist Henry Bates explored the jungles of Brazil in the 1840s and 1850s, he reported seeing a tarantula eating a bird, a scene just like the one "recorded long ago by Madame Merian."

Maria Sibylla's dynamic picture of organisms attacking each other depicts the universal struggle for survival in the jungle and was one of the first drawings to show part of a rain-forest ecosystem.

Guava Tree with Huntsman Spider, Orb Weaver Spider, Leaf-Cutter Ants, Army Ants, Cockroach, Tarantulas, and Hummingbird from *The Insects of Surinam* by Maria Sibylla Merian

Cardinal's Guard with Idomeneus Giant Owl Butterfly and Paper Wasp from *The Insects of Surinam* by Maria Sibylla Merian

Though trekking through the jungle was difficult, it revealed amazing new insects. Maria Sibylla wrote, "In January 1701 I entered the forest of Surinam to see if I could discover anything. . . . I found here a lovely, large red caterpillar, which had on each segment three blue beads, and on each bead a black feather. I intended to feed it with the leaves of this tree, but it first cocooned itself and then turned into such a strange pupa, so that I am not certain whether I found the right food for it or not. On 14 January such a lovely butterfly emerged."

Grapes with Gaudy Sphinx Moth from *The Insects of Surinam* by Maria Sibylla Merian

Maria Sibylla's servants brought her caterpillars and maggots and told her what kinds of creatures would develop from them. She remarked in her study book, after watching a disappointing brown moth emerge from the chrysalis of a colorful caterpillar, that often "the most beautiful and curious caterpillars are transformed into the simplest creatures and the simplest caterpillars into the most beautiful owl moths and diurnal butterflies."

Maria Sibylla bred the creatures she received and took notes on their development. With insect eggs and cocoons in front of her, and insects buzzing around her, she drew directly from life, making small sketches that she and Dorothea painted in the colors that matched what they saw. Then Maria Sibylla arranged these drawings in the sequence of each caterpillar's metamorphosis. Her fascination with living things was as fresh as it had been when she was a girl raising silkworms. Even when Surinam's insects annoyed her, they interested her:

When I painted, [wasps] flew before my eyes and hummed around my head. Near my paint-box they built a nest out of mud, which was as round as if it had been made on a potter's wheel; it stood on a small base over which they made a cover of mud to protect the interior from anything unsuitable. The wasps bored a small hole in it for them to crawl in and out. Every day I saw them carry in small caterpillars, doubtless as nourishment for themselves and for their young or worms, just as the ants do. Eventually, when their company became too troublesome, I chased them away by breaking up their house, which allowed me to see all that they had made.

Ready to see for herself where and how Surinam's animals grew in nature, Maria Sibylla ventured into the jungle. She collected cocoons and observed the behavior of ants and spiders. She was delighted by colorful parrots and fascinated by lizards and snakes. She took notes, made drawings, and brought living specimens of plants and animals back to her house to

Shoreline Purslane with Common Surinam Toad

from *The Insects of Surinam* by Maria Sibylla Merian

This toad, also called the Pipa pipa, was an important discovery. Maria Sibylla was the first to describe its unusual reproductive process. After fertilization, the eggs become embedded in the mother's back. The larvae develop into tadpoles inside pockets in the skin. Later, as shown on the right, tiny, fully developed toads emerge.

study and paint. She spent time observing the connections among living things: what insects ate which plants; what animals ate which insects; what trees sheltered which animals. She drew pictures in her study book that reflected not only what animals and plants looked like but how they developed and what roles they played in their ecosystems.

Ever the businesswoman, Maria Sibylla also kept an eye out for plants and insects that might be useful or profitable. When she found a white plant resembling tobacco, she had it dug up and brought back to her garden. She discovered a green caterpillar

Watermelon with Slug Moth from *The Insects of Surinam* by Maria Sibylla Merian

Maria Sibylla wrote that the flesh of the watermelon, which melts in the mouth, is tasty, healthy, and refreshing for the sick. She often found on the watermelon and also the cucumber plant this colorful caterpillar, with a green body and "sticky skin over the legs like a snail." Instead of legs these caterpillars have suckers that enable them to glide like a snail rather than walk.

Spectacled Caiman with False Coral Snake by Maria Sibylla Merian or Dorothea Graff, about 1701–5

During their time in Surinam, Maria Sibylla and Dorothea made many paintings of amphibians and reptiles. Some were published in the first edition of *The Insects of Surinam*, but others, like this one, were saved for a separate book on reptiles that was never completed. Some scholars think Dorothea painted most of the reptiles while her mother was concentrating on Surinam's insects.

Pomelo with Green-Banded Urania Butterfly from
The Insects of Surinam by Maria Sibylla Merian

From the huge array of plants and creatures Maria
Sibylla encountered in the New World, she often
chose to paint those that might be useful to humans.
Her descriptions usually mentioned whether the
plants were edible and, if so, how they should be prepared and whether the natives or Europeans ate them.
About this citrus fruit she wrote: "This fruit is less
sweet than the orange and not as sour as the lemon.
The peel and the flesh are tougher than in either of
these two, and that makes this fruit tastier."

Pomegranate with Lantern Flies and Cicada from
The Insects of Surinam by Maria Sibylla Merian

Maria Sibylla did sometimes make mistakes. Here she
placed cicadas and lantern flies together because, as
she wrote, "The Indians have assured me that these
flies [cicadas] develop into the so-called lantern flies
. . . shown here." She drew a composite picture with
the head and thorax of a lantern fly and the abdomen
and wings of a cicada (bottom), perhaps based on
verbal accounts. This insect does not exist. Though
she usually drew insects from life, it may be one of
the "exceptions" she mentioned in the introduction to
The Insects of Surinam (see page 72).

with a yellow stripe that spun strong thread, which she thought might make good
silk. She sent specimens back to Amsterdam for study and for sale.

Maria Sibylla's scientific work took persistence, and she didn't always find everything she was hoping for. She noted, "One might find many more things in the jungle
if it were penetrable. But the forest is so densely overgrown with thistles and thorns
that I had to send my slaves ahead with axes in hand so that they could hack an opening for me to be able to get through in some way or other, which, however, was quite
difficult notwithstanding."

She also struggled with Surinam's hot climate, normally 80–90 degrees Fahren-
heit with 80–90 percent humidity year-round. The only clothing she and Dorothea
had were black dresses with high necks and long skirts, which were completely
unsuitable for the heat. They did at least have bonnets and veils to protect their faces
from the sun. Maria Sibylla would later write to a friend in Nuremberg, "The heat in
this country is staggering, so that one can do no work at all without great difficulty."

Sweet Cherry with Morpho Butterfly from *The Insects of Surinam* by Maria Sibylla Merian

Bellyache Bush with Giant Sphinx Moth and Linnaeus's Joker Butterfly from *The Insects of Surinam* by Maria Sibylla Merian

The giant sphinx moth, shown on the right, is the only insect in South America with a proboscis long enough to reach the nectar of the rare ghost orchid, and so it is the endangered flower's only pollinator. Maria Sibylla noted that after feeding, the moth rolls the proboscis into a ball under its head. She shows the caterpillar of the sphinx moth eating the leaves of a bellyache bush. Its leaves and seeds were used by the natives to treat stomach ailments—hence the plant's common name.

For two years, with Dorothea's help and companionship, Maria Sibylla pursued her scientific investigations in Surinam. She had planned to stay longer, perhaps as long as five years, but she became very ill with a disease that caused fever and made the heat even more unbearable. It was probably malaria, from a mosquito bite. "I did not find in that country," she later wrote, "a suitable opportunity to carry out the insect studies I had hoped to do, as the climate there is very hot. The heat caused me great problems, and thus I found myself compelled to return home sooner than I anticipated." To a friend she wrote about her trip, "I almost had to pay for it with my life."

In the spring of 1701 Maria Sibylla prepared to leave South America. She had enough sketches and observations in her study book to more than fill *The Insects of Surinam* volume she was planning, and she had collected numerous insect, animal, and plant specimens. The specimens would serve as models for the Surinam book, and they would also prove to skeptical Europeans that all the unusual creatures Maria Sibylla had drawn in her study book were not too strange to be real. Some she would sell to her network of collectors, and in this way recover part of the cost of the expedition. Maria Sibylla and Dorothea packed up live specimens and preserved others pinned to boards, dried in wooden boxes, or sealed in jars of brandy. A native woman who had been working for the pair accompanied them to Amsterdam to help with the new book.

Maria Sibylla's illness made the three-month voyage home even more difficult. Dorothea cared for her mother as best she could. Despite the rolling sea, cramped quarters, poor diet, and the disappointment of having to leave earlier than planned, Maria Sibylla was still not sorry that she had embarked on this journey. She had accomplished her goal of studying and painting tropical insects in their natural surroundings, and she had fulfilled any dreams she had of travel and adventure. Now she had to get well, so she could publish her work and show the world her discoveries.

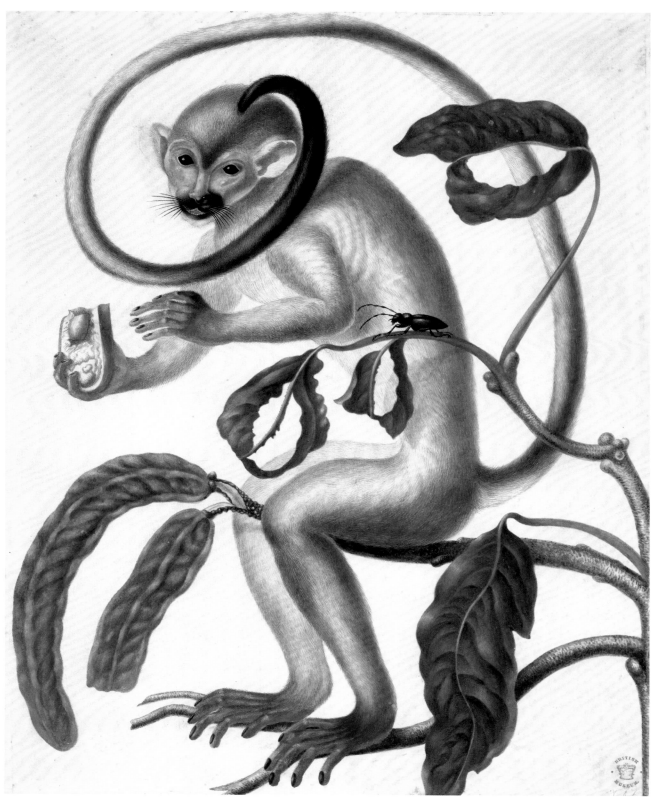

Shimbillo Tree with Squirrel Monkey by Maria Sibylla Merian, 1701–5

Chapter five
Sharing the Wonder

"Many are amazing things which have never been seen before."

Maria Sibylla Merian

When Maria Sibylla arrived back in Amsterdam, she was a celebrity. Her dangerous journey in the name of science had made her famous, especially among artists and naturalists. Botanists and collectors were excited to see what was in the crates from South America. There were caterpillars that Maria Sibylla had kept alive on the voyage; she had lizard eggs, snakes, butterflies, lantern flies, hummingbirds, flower bulbs, and even a crocodile preserved in alcohol.

As her health gradually improved, Maria Sibylla began the huge task of sorting through her sketches and notes and creating the artwork for her Surinam book. "I am painting everything with the plants and creatures life size," she wrote in her study book. "Many are amazing things which have never been seen before." Her paintings of insects, animals, and exotic plants had the scientific community buzzing. "Now that I had returned to Holland and several nature-lovers had seen my drawings, they pressured me eagerly to have them printed. They were of the opinion that this was the first and most unusual work ever painted in America."

Publishing her Surinam book would be Maria Sibylla's greatest achievement, and it was the largest project she had ever attempted. It required teamwork and extra assistants. Johanna and Dorothea helped their mother with drawing and painting. Maria Sibylla did not make her own printing plates this time but hired three print-makers to do the engraving. She supervised their work closely.

To pay for all of this, Maria Sibylla had to find subscribers—people who were willing to give her money for the book in advance. Twelve individuals agreed to this arrangement, and they were promised hand-painted deluxe editions. Less expensive versions in black and white would also be available for purchase.

Sweet Potato and Parakeet Plant with Melon Worm, Pickleworm, and Leaf-Footed Bug from *The Insects of Surinam* by Maria Sibylla Merian

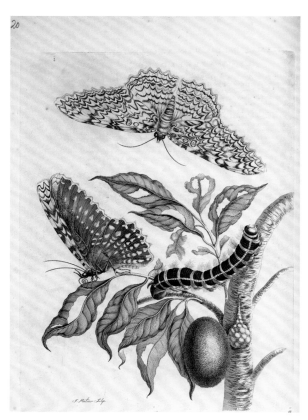

Gummi Guttae Tree and White Witch Moth from *The Insects of Surinam* by Maria Sibylla Merian

In preparing the plates for *The Insects of Surinam*, Maria Sibylla and her daughters sometimes used a technique called counterproofing that would produce two prints of the same drawing at almost the same time. The first one (left) was printed directly from the copper plate. The second (right), called the counterproof, was made from the first. A clean sheet of paper was pressed against the first print while the ink was still wet. The two prints are mirror images of each other. However, with fainter printed lines and hand-coloring, the image on the right looks more like an original painting than a print.

Maria Sibylla and Dorothea had seen gummi guttae trees at the plantations they visited along the rivers of Surinam. Their bark was white and striped, like a birch tree, and planters grew them to be able to harvest their resin. When they stripped the bark off the tree, the tree "bled" a gummy substance that was, wrote Maria Sibylla, "known to all who use paint." This gummy substance was a resin or glue that, when mixed with a dry pigment and water, turned it into paint.

Banana Flower with Bulls-Eye Moth from *The Insects of Surinam* by Maria Sibylla Merian

For some of the deluxe editions, Maria Sibylla used a method called counter-proofing. The printer placed a newly printed sheet against a blank sheet and ran it through the printing press a second time, while the ink was still wet. Now there were two prints instead of just one. Even better, the counterproofs had lighter inked outlines than the first prints, so they looked hand-drawn rather than printed. This was an innovative technique for illustrations.

In 1705 Maria Sibylla published *The Insects of Surinam*, with text available in Dutch or Latin. She described the book this way in the introduction:

The book consists of ninety studies of caterpillars, worms, and maggots, showing how they change in color and form once they had shed their skins, or cuticle, and are finally transformed into butterflies, moths, beetles, bees, and flies. All these little creatures I have placed on the plants, flowers, and fruits that provide their special food. To them I have added the development of the West Indian spiders, ants, snakes, lizards, and the rare toads and frogs. These were all observed by me in America and drawn from life, with only a few exceptions, which I have added based on what the Indians told me.

Jasmine with Ello Yellow Sphinx Moth and Amazon Tree Boa from *The Insects of Surinam* by Maria Sibylla Merian

Maria Sibylla noted that numerous lizards, iguanas, and snakes lived under sweet-smelling jasmine bushes. She found this Amazon tree boa, which she called a "lovely and rare snake," under a jasmine plant, although its usual habitat is on high tree branches. These snakes are nocturnal and their eyes have a reflective membrane that makes them appear to shine at night. Although it is abundant, this boa is rarely seen. It helps to hide itself by forming a coil and pulling its head inside. It is remarkable that Maria Sibylla spotted this one.

Nightshade with Automeris Moth and Molippa Moth from *The Insects of Surinam* by Maria Sibylla Merian

About these moths Maria Sibylla wrote, "Seen through a magnifying glass, both moths appear to have hair like that on honey bears." She observed that the yellow-and-black caterpillar (below) normally stayed in a group, lying head-to-tail in a circle. The red caterpillar with yellow stripes (above) has long hairs that can sting.

The book had sixty illustrations on large pages about fourteen inches wide and twenty-one inches tall. As she had done in *The Caterpillar Book,* Maria Sibylla showed the stages of metamorphosis, and opposite each picture she presented the scientific observations she had written in her study book. She also included some of the information given to her by native women about their uses of plants, flowers, and insects for food and medicine. The native woman who came with Maria Sibylla to Amsterdam helped with these descriptions. They recorded many details about the lives of native people in South America—fascinating reading for untraveled Europeans and for later historical anthropologists.

Nothing quite like *The Insects of Surinam* had ever been seen before. The richness of detail and scientific accuracy of Maria Sibylla's observations attracted praise from artists and scientists all across Europe. The London botanist James Petiver wrote a letter telling Maria Sibylla that "All most curious persons in England" had

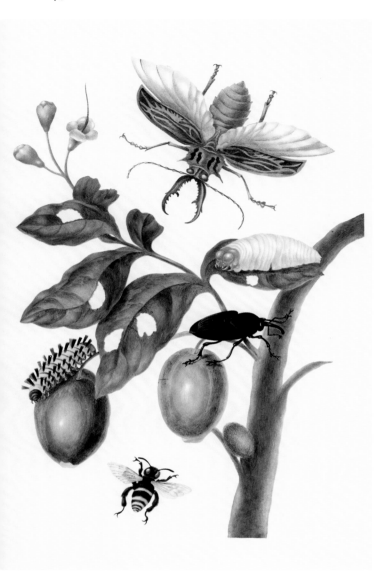

Genipa with Bee, Long-Horn Beetle, and Palm Weevil from *The Insects of Surinam* by Maria Sibylla Merian

Maria Sibylla noted that the native people used these plants and insects for various purposes, though not the ones that might be expected. The fruit was not eaten, but its juice was made into a black dye used for body decoration. Sap from the tree was rubbed onto itchy scalps to treat worm infestations. The fat white worm at the upper right normally lived on palm trees, which were too big for Maria Sibylla to draw life size on the page. She included it here because it metamorphosed into the interesting black beetle shown underneath, and also because these worms were considered a delicacy by the natives, who roasted them over coals before eating them.

high praise for her book, including the bishop of London and the archbishop of Canterbury. Maria Sibylla thought about publishing a version in English just so she could send it to the queen of England. "It is reasonable for a woman to make such a gift to a person of the same sex," she wrote. She never did print the book in English, but in 1754 the future King George III purchased a deluxe edition of *The Insects of Surinam* in Latin. It is now in the Royal Collection at Windsor Castle.

Cassava with Common Tegu and White Peacock Butterfly from *The Insects of Surinam* by Maria Sibylla Merian

According to Maria Sibylla, the tegu lizard grows "to the size of a crocodile" and lays eggs "as big as turkey eggs." Natives and Europeans living in Surinam made bread from cassava root, which had to be grated, squeezed, and cooked thoroughly in order to rid it of poisonous liquid.

Cone Shells, Harp Shells, and Butterfly Shells by Maria Sibylla Merian, 1705

The Insects of Surinam had made Maria Sibylla famous for her accurate drawings of nature. When an Amsterdam publisher wanted to print a catalogue of shells and other natural specimens from Indonesia, he asked her for assistance. These shells were from the collection of the naturalist Georg Eberhard Rumpf, who became blind and then died before he could complete his catalogue, called *The Amboinese Curiosity Cabinet*.

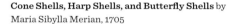

Maria Sibylla's artistic and scientific achievements brought her fame and respect, but they did not earn her a fortune. She continued to sell prints and paintings and to trade in exotic animal specimens, helped by Dorothea's new husband—a surgeon named Philip Hendriks who often sailed with Dutch merchants on their voyages. Dorothea married him shortly after her return from Surinam.

Maria Sibylla's growing reputation attracted the interest of the publisher Frans Halma. He was eager to produce a book called *The Amboinese Curiosity Cabinet* written by Georg Eberhard Rumpf, a German naturalist who had been an agent for the Dutch East India Company. Halma asked for Maria Sibylla's help with illustrations of the Indonesian shells, rocks, fossils, and sea animals collected by Rumpf. Maria Sibylla might have accepted this assignment because she needed the income. It is possible that Dorothea helped her mother with these paintings.

The Art of Maria Sibylla Merian's Daughters

Maria Sibylla taught her daughters to be artists. All three women painted in a similar style, so it can be hard to tell which woman really painted which pictures. Sometimes Johanna or Dorothea finished paintings that their mother had started, and sometimes Maria Sibylla signed paintings that were actually made by her daughters. She was, after all, the famous artist, and paintings with her signature brought the highest prices. It was not unusual for master painters to give some of their work to assistants and to sign paintings and charge the highest prices to benefit the family enterprise.

Still, Johanna developed her own style and eventually pursued painting independently. Her pictures of flowers often seem similar to her mother's, but they are slightly less scientific. Compare two paintings of a vermilion lily, one by Maria Sibylla and one by Johanna. Johanna's is less complex, with softer lines and not a single imperfection. Maria Sibylla shows some of the leaves turning brown, with holes made by nibbling insects. Johanna was more interested in beauty and less concerned with painting directly from nature.

Vermilion Lily by Maria Sibylla Merian, 1691–99

Vermilion Lily by Johanna Herolt, 1695–99

Dorothea had her own style too. Art historians consider her work less refined than Maria Sibylla's, but she was very good at capturing intricate details. She helped her mother with many paintings from Surinam, where they worked together for two years. This image of a water hyacinth is thought to have been made by Dorothea.

Portrait of Maria Sibylla Merian painted by Jacob Houbraken, 1717, after a drawing by Georg Gsell

Georg Gsell, a Swiss artist living in Amsterdam, drew Maria Sibylla's portrait, and a later artist turned the drawing into this painting. Maria Sibylla is shown surrounded by the things she loved: books and an inkwell with a feather pen for writing; her drawings of flowers, insects, shells, and a paintbrush for painting; a magnifying glass; a globe; and, of course, a live plant and a butterfly. The statuettes behind her personify Fame (left) and the Dutch Republic (right).

Water Hyacinth and Veined Tree Frog from *The Insects of Surinam* by Maria Sibylla Merian, attributed to Dorothea Graff

Maria Sibylla had many other things to do. She updated the first two volumes of *The Caterpillar Book* and published them in Dutch, doing the translation herself. She had the third volume to finish, and because she had many unpublished drawings from her trip to Surinam, she planned another Surinam book that would feature the reptiles, amphibians, and brightly colored birds of the tropics. And now that she was famous, she often had to stop what she was doing to welcome visitors who wanted to meet her and purchase paintings or rare specimens for their collections.

A scholar who visited Maria Sibylla in 1711, when she was sixty-four years old, described her as lively, hardworking, and courteous, and her house as full of drawings—of insects, plants, fruit, and at least fifty watercolors of the animals of Surinam.

Cardinal's Flower with Brown Meadow Butterfly
from *The Caterpillar Book* by Maria Sibylla Merian
Maria Sibylla found this caterpillar in Amsterdam.
She observed its metamorphosis to pupa and then
butterfly, as shown here.

A Swiss artist named Georg Gsell drew her portrait at about the same time, and he showed her seated among her drawings.

Later that year Johanna moved to Surinam with her husband, who had been offered an administrative post there, and her young daughter, Maria Abigail. Johanna lived in Paramaribo the rest of her life, though she may have returned on extended visits to work with her mother again. Dorothea's husband died, and she remained in Amsterdam with Maria Sibylla.

On May 28, 1711, Maria Sibylla made her last entry in her study book. It was a drawing of a moth emerging from its cocoon. Her groundbreaking study of insect metamorphosis, which she began at age thirteen, had endured for fifty-one years. In all that time, Maria Sibylla never lost her enthusiasm, her curiosity, or her sense of wonder.

Maria Sibylla still had every intention of publishing the third volume of *The Caterpillar Book*. In the preface to *The Insects of Surinam* she had written, "If God gives me health and life enough, I intend to augment the observations I have made in Germany with the additions of those from Friesland and Holland and to publish them in Latin and Dutch." But in 1715 she suffered a stroke, and she could no longer work. With Johanna in Surinam, it was now up to Dorothea to finish the third volume for her mother.

Dorothea added fifty new plates, based on drawings by Maria Sibylla, Johanna, and herself. She combined them with the first two volumes in the same way that Maria Sibylla had combined the three sets of flower prints in *The New Book of Flowers*. But in January 1717, just before the complete *Caterpillar Book* was published, Maria Sibylla died at the age of sixty-nine.

She had lived an extraordinary life. Fiercely independent, she pursued her artistic and scientific vision despite financial difficulties, traditional attitudes that restricted women's choices, and the responsibility of raising her daughters by herself. With determination and patience, ingenuity and imagination, she studied and recorded the lives of insects, reptiles, and amphibians, and she pioneered the field of scientific illustration. Today her work continues to inspire artists, scientists, and everyday people, everywhere, to explore the rich diversity and wonder of the natural world that she so loved and worked so tirelessly to reveal.

Garden Iris with Iris Borer Moth from
The Caterpillar Book by Maria Sibylla Merian

Maria Sibylla found these white caterpillars eating
blue irises. She noted that the young larva of the
iris borer moth crawled up the stem from the earth,
tunneled to the base of the leaves, and then molted
into a small pupa. The next year it turned into a gray
"nocturnal butterfly," her term for a moth.

Fox Moth and July High Flier Moth from
The Caterpillar Book by Maria Sibylla Merian

Here Maria Sibylla shows both the male (left) and
female (right) of the fox moth caterpillar, seen with
its oval cocoon on the branch just below.

Epilogue

In January 1717, the same month that Maria Sibylla died, agents of Czar Peter the Great of Russia purchased nearly three hundred of her watercolor paintings and her study book. Peter was building a new Western-style city—St. Petersburg, named after himself. He wanted to make it "a second Amsterdam."

As a young man, in 1697–98, Peter had visited Amsterdam in disguise, posing as a workman to learn how the Dutch built their ships and windmills. He did not meet Maria Sibylla or her daughters, but he did study painting with their friend Frederik Ruysch. In 1716–17 Peter returned to Amsterdam, looking for the finest art and objects for his palace in St. Petersburg. He gave instructions for the purchase of works by Maria Sibylla Merian. These he would display in his new room of wonder, where he wanted to showcase the diversity of the entire natural world. Peter hired the artist Georg Gsell to advise him on his purchases and transport them back to Russia. Georg, who had known Maria Sibylla and Dorothea for some time, asked Dorothea to marry him. In 1718 the couple moved to St. Petersburg.

Before she left Amsterdam, Dorothea signed a contract with the bookseller Johannes Oosterwijk, agreeing to sell him her mother's books, including "all the Surinamese and European insect and flower books" and "the plates, impressions and letterpress, both colored and uncolored." Oosterwijk published a Latin edition of *The Caterpillar Book* in 1718 and then several editions of *The Insects of Surinam*.

Dorothea ensured that her mother's lifework would remain in print and that people would continue to be inspired by the fascinating beauty of nature. In

Nettle with Red Admiral Butterfly, Ichneumon Wasp, and Chalcid Wasp from *The Caterpillar Book* by Maria Sibylla Merian

Прослектъ пб низъ по Невъ ръкъ между зимнимъ
Ея Императорскаго Величества домомъ и Академиею Наукъ

Vüe des bords de la Neva en descendant la riviere entre le Palais
d'hyver de Sa Majesté Imperiale & les batimens de l'Academie des Sciences

Banks of the Neva River in St. Petersburg

from *Plan of St. Petersburg and Its Avenues* by Ivan Sokolov and Mikhail Makhaev, 1753

The Imperial Academy of Sciences, a building with a central tower, is visible on the river's right bank.

St. Petersburg, Dorothea colored special editions of her mother's books that she had brought with her, and she taught Russian students how to draw from nature. Peter put her in charge of decorating his room of wonder, which later became the Imperial Academy of Sciences and then the Soviet Academy of Sciences. After the Soviet Union dissolved, it was renamed the Russian Academy of Sciences, and its archive still holds many drawings of plants by Dorothea and her students. Dorothea and Georg Gsell had three sons and a daughter, none of whom became artists.

In the first half of the eighteenth century, as more editions of her books and paintings were published, Maria Sibylla's fame grew. Collectors cherished her artworks, and many were preserved in museums, archives, and scientific institutions. Biologists who had never traveled to the Americas used her drawings and descriptions to classify and name insects that they could not see for themselves. Botanical and zoological illustrators imitated her artistic style, and following her example, they began paying attention to the connections among plants, insects, and other animals in nature.

But as scientific study advanced and became more specialized, Maria Sibylla and many other naturalists of her day were largely forgotten. The professional scientists of the nineteenth century dismissed those of earlier eras as outdated amateurs, and they criticized Maria Sibylla's work because they didn't believe that a seventeenth-century woman could have produced reliable scientific data.

Then, in 1974, the Soviet Academy of Sciences published fifty of Maria Sibylla's watercolors, followed two years later by a copy of her study book. These inspired new interest in the work of this astonishing artist and scientist. Curators

Naming Plants and Animals

In *The Caterpillar Book* and *The Insects of Surinam*, Maria Sibylla used common, everyday words like "silkworm" and "wasp" to identify insects. In her descriptions she sometimes used fanciful terms—a pupa was a "date pit" and a butterfly a "summer bird."

At the time, there was no standardized scientific terminology for plants and animals, as there is today. About thirty years after Maria Sibylla published *The Insects of Surinam*, Carl Linnaeus, a Swedish botanist and medical doctor, began to devise a universal classification system for all the organisms of the natural world. It is called binomial nomenclature, and with modifications, it is still used today. Linnaeus organized all plants and animals using five levels: kingdom, class, order, genus, and species. He gave each organism a two-part Latin name, one identifying the genus and one the species. He published his classifications in *Systema Naturae* beginning in 1735 and in *Species Plantarum* in 1753. Linnaeus's system became the world's scientific standard.

For plants and insects from the jungles of Surinam that Linnaeus never saw for himself, he relied on Maria Sibylla's drawings. He had never examined a lantern fly, for example, but he trusted Maria Sibylla's report and named it in Latin *Fulgora laternaria* (lantern bearer). He used Maria Sibylla's books to describe the tarantula, along with fifty-six other animals and thirty-nine plants. In his references to her work he abbreviated her name as *Mer.*, using *Mer. surin.* to cite *The Insects of Surinam*, and *Mer. eur.* for *European Insects*, the title of a later printing of *The Caterpillar Book*.

In binomial nomenclature, the name of the individual who discovered a species is preserved. Today, more than a dozen species of insects, animals, and plants; a genus of mantises; and a genus of flowering plants are named in honor of Maria Sibylla.

Coffee Senna with Split-Banded Owlet Butterfly from *The Insects of Surinam* by Maria Sibylla Merian

One of the species named after Maria Sibylla is the split-banded owlet butterfly, given the scientific name *Opsiphanes cassina merianae* by a German scientist in 1902. It was one of the many insects first recorded by Maria Sibylla in Surinam.

Frontispiece for the 1719 edition of *The Insects of Surinam* engraved by J. Oosterwijk

This fanciful picture was created for an edition of *The Insects of Surinam* that was published after Maria Sibylla's death. She is shown seated on the left looking down at her own book. Behind the book a pineapple, her favorite fruit, grows in a pot. Six cherubs, or putti, help her by sorting and storing her collection of specimens. Behind her a Roman-style arch frames a landscape of Surinam as it appeared after cultivation by European colonists. In the distance is another picture of Maria Sibylla; she is collecting butterflies in a field on the banks of a river.

searched museum collections and mounted international art exhibitions so they could reintroduce Maria Sibylla to the world. Scholars—including those in the new field of women's studies—researched her life and work, writing more than two dozen books about her in less than twenty years. Publishers printed new editions of her books.

There was renewed appreciation for Maria Sibylla as a scientist. Entomologists found they could identify almost every one of her caterpillars and were amazed at the accuracy of her drawings. Ecologists discovered that their profession had a forerunner from long ago. Environmentalists found inspiration for their continued efforts to preserve the teeming diversity of life on this planet.

In recent decades, Maria Sibylla Merian has once again been recognized for her achievements and her role in history. Among other things, she has had her picture on banknotes and stamps, had a scientific research ship named after her, and been the subject of a play. She was honored with a Google Doodle on April 2, 2013—her 366th birthday.

Maria Sibylla Merian German Banknote

Germany, the country of Maria Sibylla's birth, issued a banknote in her honor in 1991. The 500 deutsche mark note shows a portrait of Maria Sibylla on the front and a dandelion with the pale tussock moth and caterpillar on the back. Issued before Germany converted to the euro, the note is no longer in circulation.

Maria Sibylla Merian U.S. Postage Stamps

In 1997 the United States Postal Service issued stamps illustrated with a citron and a pineapple from *The Insects of Surinam*. The stamps were intended to honor not only Maria Sibylla but also the contributions of women artists throughout history.

Green Iguana by Maria Sibylla Merian, 1701–10

On April 2, 2013, this painting was adapted for a Google Doodle in celebration of Maria Sibylla's 366th birthday.

Organisms Named in Honor of Maria Sibylla Merian

Bird
Saxicola torquatus sibilla (Madagascan stonechat)

Insects
Erinnyis merianae (Cuban sphinx moth)
Eulaema meriana (orchid bee)
Evagetes merianae van der Smissen (spider wasp)
Heliconius melpomene meriana (common postman butterfly)
Opsiphanes cassina merianae (split-banded owlet butterfly)
Plisthenes merianae (no common name)
The genus *Sibylla* (mantises)

Lizard
Salvator merianae (Argentine black-and-white tegu)

Plants
The genus *Meriana* (flowering plants)
Watsonia meriana (bulbil bugle-lily)

Snail
Coquandiella meriana (no common name)

Spiders
Avicularia merianae (bird-eating spider)
Metellina merianae (no common name)

Toad
Rhinella merianae (cane toad)

Glossary

amphibian
A smooth-skinned, cold-blooded animal that lives in or near water.

Arawak
One of the native peoples of **Surinam**.

binder
A substance mixed with the **pigment** in **watercolor** paint to make it stick to a surface.

binomial nomenclature
A system of two-part Latin names used to classify organisms in the natural world.

biodiversity
The variety of living organisms within a specific area.

Carib
One of the native peoples of **Surinam**.

caterpillar
The wormlike juvenile form of a butterfly or moth.

chrysalis
The hardened body of a **pupa**, sometimes contained within a spun silken **cocoon**.

cinnabar
An orange-red **pigment** derived from a mineral of the same name.

cochineal
An **insect** from which carmine red **pigment** is derived.

cocoon
The silken casing that is spun by a caterpillar to surround the **pupa**.

colony
An outpost in one part of the world that is controlled by people from another country.

composition
A work of art and the arrangement of elements within it.

counterproof
A print made by pressing a freshly printed page onto a clean sheet of paper or **vellum**.

curiosity cabinet: *see* **room of wonder**

cuticle
A **caterpillar**'s outer skin, which serves as an external skeleton that is periodically shed.

ecologist
A scientist who explores the relationship between organisms and their environment.

ecosystem
The living and nonliving elements in a shared environment.

embroidery
The craft of sewing colored thread onto cloth using different types of stitches to create patterns and pictures.

engraving
The process and product of carving a design into a hard surface, such as a copper **plate**, and then making prints of the design.

entomologist
A scientist who studies **insects**.

gum arabic
A sticky substance collected from acacia trees and used as a **binder**.

insect
A small **invertebrate** with a body formed of three parts, with six legs and usually two pairs of wings.

invertebrate
An animal that has no backbone.

Labadists
A Protestant Christian community, founded in Holland in 1669 by Jean de Labadie, that followed a strict religious lifestyle.

lapis lazuli
A blue **pigment** derived from a mineral of the same name.

larva
The immature stage in the life of a butterfly or moth, commonly called a **caterpillar**.

magnifying glass
A lens used to enlarge a view of an object.

metamorphosis
The changes in the life cycle of an **insect** from egg to adult.

molting
The process by which an **insect** sheds its outer skin.

parasite
An organism that lives and feeds on another organism.

parasitoid
An organism that lives and feeds on another organism, eventually killing it.

pigment
A powder ground from natural materials and used as a coloring agent.

plate
A hard surface into which a design is carved to produce prints, which are known as plates or **engravings**.

predator
An organism that feeds on and kills other organisms.

pupa
A nonfeeding and usually nonactive stage of **metamorphosis** between the **caterpillar** and adult **insect**.

Reformation
The historical period when Protestant Christianity broke away from the Roman Catholic Church.

reptile
A scaly, cold-blooded animal.

room of wonder (also called **curiosity cabinet**)
A space designed for the display of multiple natural and manmade objects collected for scientific or artistic reasons.

scientific method
A process of observing, recording, testing, and explaining the natural world.

silk
Fiber from the **cocoon** of a silkworm that can be spun into thread for use in creating cloth.

specimen
A sample collected for scientific study or display.

spider
A small **invertebrate** with a body formed of two parts, eight legs, and a pair of pincers or fangs.

spontaneous generation
The outdated theory that living organisms could be generated by nonliving matter.

still life
A work of art with a static arrangement of natural and manmade objects.

Surinam
A country on the northeast coast of South America that was once a Dutch **colony**.

tachinid
A type of fly that is a **parasitoid**.

Treaty of Breda
A 1667 agreement that ended a war between Holland and England and gave control of **Surinam** to the Dutch.

vellum
A sheet of animal skin that is prepared as a surface on which to write or create a work of art.

watercolor
A mixture of a **pigment** and **binder** in water, used as a medium for creating a work of art.

women's studies
An interdisciplinary academic field with a focus on the role of women in society.

Acknowledgments

It is a pleasure to begin by thanking Lee Pomeroy for inspiring my interest in Surinam. Next, I thank Laura Schor for suggesting both that I write a book for my grandchildren and that I discuss the project with Natalie Zemon Davis, an expert on Maria Sibylla Merian, who immediately expressed her enthusiasm for the project. I am grateful to the Family History Research Group, who read the manuscript more than once, and especially to the late Barbara McManus for contributing her photograph of the coin of the Roman Sibyl.

Thanks to Jeyaraney Kathirithamby, who eagerly accepted my invitation to contribute to the scientific content of the book, and to her husband, Malcolm Davies, who translated entomological texts from Old German and Dutch.

I am grateful to Kay Etheridge for her comments on the manuscript and for sharing her current research on the three volumes of *The Caterpillar Book*. I am also indebted to Lee Foster for practical advice on agriculture and on the artistic portrayal of plants and their pests. Thanks to Guido Castillo of the Museo Entomológico y de Historia Natural de Vicuña, Chile, for opening his "rooms of wonder" to Lee Foster and me.

This book ranges through many fields, including women's history, art history, history of science, costume history, and Dutch history. I gratefully acknowledge the help of many experts in these fields, especially Larissa Bonfannte, Daniel Margocsy, Elizabeth McFadden, and Eric Jan Sluijter.

Thanks are due to Arader Galleries, the Frick Art Reference Library, the Frits Lugt Collection, the Getty Research Institute, and the National Museum of Women in the Arts for facilitating my research. I am delighted to thank my students Branko van Oppen de Ruiter, Walter Penrose, and Georgia Tsouvala for the magnificent and timely gift of M. Van Delft and H. Mulder, *Metamorphosis insectorum Surinamensium*. I am also grateful to Branko van Oppen de Ruiter for translating botanical Dutch and offering advice on navigating Dutch online sources.

Thanks are due to editor Ann Grogg for her supreme efforts on behalf of this book, to Mary Batten and Leo Torrocha for their skillful help in preparing the manuscript, and to Gregory Dobie for his precise proofreading and his work on the glossary. Once again, it is a pleasure to thank John Adams for his incisive and learned comments.

My thanks also go to librarian Madeline Bryant and educator Kim Parfitt for their valuable critiques. Numerous young readers in New York and California read the book as it developed. Among these I single out for their generous comments: Carly Fisher, Kenan House, Danielle Manos, Tabitha Mettler, Avery Nicholson, Jesse Pomeroy, Talia Pomeroy, and Angelina Shoemaker.

At Getty Publications, my sincere thanks go to publisher Kara Kirk for her ongoing support, Kurt Hauser for his scintillating book design, Victoria Gallina for supervising production, and Pam Moffat and Pauline Lopez for coordinating the images. I appreciate the assistance given at various times by Rachel Barth, Jackie Hwang, and Nicole Kim. I would also like to thank the enthusiastic marketing staff: Maureen Winter, Miranda Sklaroff, and Kim Westad. Special thanks to curator Stephanie Schrader for her support of this project and for her expert comments on Dutch art history.

It is a pleasure to thank my daughter Jordana Pomeroy for introducing me to senior editor Elizabeth Nicholson at Getty Publications, who has shown patience, passion, and imagination in editing this multifaceted book. I am also grateful to my son, Jeremy Pomeroy, for kind counsel during the four years of this book's gestation. Finally, I thank my beloved and much-lamented daughter Alexandra Pomeroy for her grace and intelligence in interpreting and mediating between the worlds of adults and children.

Sarah B. Pomeroy
Sag Harbor, New York, 2017

I give my first thanks to Malcolm Davies for translating Maria Sibylla's observations from Old German, Dutch, and French, which allowed me to identify and write about the animals and plants in the plates and provide the scientific content for this volume.

To Sarah Pomeroy, my thanks for suggesting that we collaborate on this book.

The Bodleian Library, University of Oxford; the Dumbarton Oaks Research Library and Collection; and the Getty Research Institute all kindly gave me access to Maria Sibylla Merian's publications. I had interesting conversations about Maria Sibylla with the staff of the Adler Gallery, New York, for which I am thankful.

Richard Ovenden, Bodley's Librarian, encouraged me in my studies on Maria Sibylla. David Wells employed his biology expertise to carefully proofread the scientific captions and sidebars, which I much appreciate. I had long discussions with Alan Todd regarding early microscopy, for which I am grateful. Thanks too to Katharina Schmidt-Loske, Tinde van Andel, and Hajo Gernaat for their discussions on plants and animals.

St. Hugh's College, University of Oxford, gave me assistance and support when it was most needed, for which I am very grateful.

To senior editor Elizabeth Nicholson at Getty Publications, my utmost thanks for her kind advice and guidance. Last but not least, I join Sarah Pomeroy in my thanks to editor Ann Grogg and to the Getty Publications team (as listed above) for all their marvelous work on this book.

Jeyaraney Kathirithamby
Oxford, England, 2017

Selected Bibliography

Who was Maria Sibylla Merian? She was an artist and a scientist who produced important and beautiful books, and she lived more than three hundred years ago. How do we find out about her life and work and about who she was as a person?

All the books that Maria Sibylla wrote and illustrated are available; they are listed below. Most of what Maria Sibylla wrote in her study book and her published books is about plants, animals, and insects, not about herself. She left behind some letters, which are largely about selling her paintings, books, and biological specimens. They show that she was an astute businesswoman, but they do not reveal her intimate thoughts.

Women have always been less visible than men as historical figures, so it is more difficult to find out about them. As a pioneer in the field of women's history, Sarah Pomeroy devised ways to find information about historical women in what others wrote about them and through nontraditional historical sources, including visual images. She discovered many things about Maria Sibylla in paintings. For example, in the portrait on page 13, some of Maria Sibylla's family members are dressed up as ancient Romans. Their costumes show that they wanted to present themselves as educated, cultured, and also playful. In the portrait of an older Maria Sibylla on page 79, she is portrayed as a studious woman at a desk, surrounded by books, a globe, a butterfly, sculptures referring to her public honors, and drawings of shells and flowers that call attention to her lifelong work in natural history. This depiction tells us that Maria Sibylla was considered knowledgeable and accomplished.

People's actions say a lot about them. Venturing into a jungle known to contain jaguars, crocodiles, and poisonous snakes certainly required bravery, so it is easy to deduce that Maria Sibylla was brave. Researching the times and places in which Maria Sibylla lived enhanced her story. For example, there are no written records of exactly what kind of ship she sailed on, but it is possible to learn about seventeenth-century Dutch shipping and make an educated guess.

Entomologist Jeyaraney Kathirithamby identified the insects, animals, and plants in this book using current scientific literature along with Maria Sibylla's paintings and her vivid descriptions of her subjects' various life stages. Maria Sibylla used common terms to describe organisms, some of which were later given scientific names by Linnaeus when he introduced binomial nomenclature (see page 85). After identifying the species in Maria Sibylla's engravings, Jeyaraney consulted Linnaeus's tenth edition of *Systema Naturae* for early scientific names and the *Catalogue of Life* (www.catalogueoflife.org) for the most recent, perhaps revised, scientific and common names. She added up-to-date information to Maria Sibylla's early observations and discoveries.

Below are some of the many sources consulted by the authors during the writing of this book.

Books by Maria Sibylla Merian

Some of Maria Sibylla's books were published in separate volumes that were later collected and published together as single books. Later editions may differ from first editions and might even contain additional material that was not created by Maria Sibylla. For example, the large ant on page 46 of this book was added to Maria Sibylla's floral wreath by a later engraver.

The original titles of Maria Sibylla's books have been translated and shortened here.

The New Book of Flowers

This book is Maria Sibylla's first. She published it in three parts: the first in 1675, the second in 1677, and the third in 1680. She also gathered the three parts into a single book and published it in 1680.

The Caterpillar Book

Maria Sibylla published two volumes of *The Caterpillar Book*: the first in 1679 and the second in 1683. She was still working on the third volume when she died in 1717, and it was published by her daughter Dorothea later the same year. Dorothea also produced an edition containing all three volumes. In 1718 an Amsterdam publisher purchased

the plates for all three volumes and published them together in a single book. Another edition containing all three volumes was published in 1730 with a new title: *European Insects*.

The Insects of Surinam

Maria Sibylla published one edition of *The Insects of Surinam* in 1705. She was planning a second book on the reptiles and amphibians of Surinam but was never able to complete it. Some of the later editions of *The Insects of Surinam* produced by other publishers contain extra images of reptiles, amphibians, and other animals. These pictures might have been intended for the second Surinam book, and some of them might have been painted by Dorothea.

Getty Edition

Many of the illustrations in this book are reproduced from the second edition of *The Insects of Surinam*, magnificently hand-colored near the time of its publication in 1719. The book is bound in richly gold-tooled leather along with hand-colored 1730 editions of *The Caterpillar Book* (*European Insects*) and *The New Book of Flowers*. It is held in the collection of the Getty Research Institute, Los Angeles (ID # 89-B10750).

The Insects of Surinam is digitized and viewable online at https://archive.org/details/gri_33125011169527

The Caterpillar Book is digitized and viewable online at https://archive.org/details/gri_33125008530400

Primary Sources
The following are modern printings of original books by Maria Sibylla.

Merian, Maria Sibylla. *Flowers, Butterflies and Insects: All 154 Engravings from "Erucarum Ortus."* New York: Dover, 1991.

———. *Insects of Surinam: Metamorphosis Insectorum Surinamensium.* Edited by Katharina Schmidt-Loske. Hong Kong; Cologne: Taschen, 2009.

———. *Leningrad Watercolours.* 2 vols. Edited by Ernst Ullmann. New York: Harcourt Brace Jovanovich, 1974.

———. *Maria Sibylla Merian: The St. Petersburg Watercolours.* Edited by Eckhard Hollmann, with natural history commentaries by Wolf-Dietrich Beer. Munich; New York: Prestel, 2003.

———. *Metamorphosis Insectorum Surinamensium.* 2 vols. Vol. 2 commentary by Elisabeth Rücker and William T. Stearn. London: Pion, 1980–82.

———. *Metamorphosis Insectorum Surinamensium.* Edited by Marieke van Delft and Hans Mulder. Tielt: Lannoo, 2016.

———. *New Book of Flowers.* Contributions by Thomas Bürger and Marina Heilmeyer. Munich: Prestel, 1999.

———. *Schmetterlinge, Käser und andere Insekten: Leningrader Studienbuch.* Edited by Wolf-Dietrich Beer, with commentary by Irina Lebedeva, Wolf-Dietrich Beer, and Gerrit Friese. Leipzig: Edition Leipzig, 1976.

———. *The Wondrous Transformation of Caterpillars: Fifty Engravings Selected from Erucarum Ortus (1718).* Introduction by William T. Stearn. London: Scolar Press, 1978.

Secondary Sources
These are books and articles about Maria Sibylla or topics related to her life and work.

Bates, Henry Walter. *The Naturalist on the River Amazons: A Record of Adventures, Habits of Animals, Sketches of Brazilian and Indian Life, and Aspects of Nature Under the Equator, During Eleven Years of Travel.* London: J. Murray, 1873.

Blumenthal, Hannah. "A Taste for Exotica: Maria Sibylla Merian's *Metamorphosis insectorum Surinamensium.*" *Gastronomica* 6 (2006): 44–52.

Brafman, David, and Stephanie Schrader. *Insects & Flowers: The Art of Maria Sibylla Merian.* Los Angeles: J. Paul Getty Museum, 2008.

Campos Silva, João Vitor and Fernanda de Almeida Meirelles. "A Small Homage to Maria Sibylla Merian and New Records of Spiders (Araneae: Theraphosidae) Preying on Birds." *Revista Brasileira de Ornitologia* 24 (2016): 30–33.

Cobb, Matthew. "Malpighi, Swammerdam and the Colourful Silkworm: Replication and Visual Representation in Early Modern Science." *Annals of Science* 59 (2002): 111–47.

———. "Reading and Writing *The Book of Nature*: Jan Swammerdam (1637–1680)." *Endeavour* 24 (2000): 122–28.

Etheridge, Kay. "Maria Sibylla Merian: The First Ecologist?" In *Women and Science, 17th Century to Present*, edited by V. Molinari and D. Andreolle. Newcastle upon Tyne: Cambridge Scholars Publishing, 2011.

———. "Maria Sibylla Merian and the Metamorphosis of Natural History." *Endeavour* 35 (2010): 15–21.

The Maria Sibylla Merian Society. "Books by Maria Sibylla Merian (Overview)." http://www.themariasibyllameriansociety.humanities.uva.nl/merianwork/overview-of-books-of-maria-sibylla-merian/.

Lenteren, J. C. van, and H. C. J. Godfray. "European Science in the Enlightenment and the Discovery of the Insect Parasitoid Life Cycle in The Netherlands and Great Britain." *Biological Control* 32 (2005): 12–24.

Linnaeus, Carl. *Systema Naturae*, 10th edition, 1758. http://www.biodiversitylibrary.org/item/10277.

Nutting, Catherine M. "Crossing Disciplines: The Fruitful Duality of Maria Sibylla Merian's Artistic and Naturalist Inheritances." *Dutch Crossing* 35 (2011): 137–47.

Parvavisini-Gebert, Lizabeth. "Maria Sibylla Merian: The Dawn of Field Ecology in the Forests of Surinam, 1699–1701." *Review: Literature and Arts of the Americas* 45 (2012): 10–20.

Reitsma, Ella. *Maria Sibylla Merian & Daughters: Women of Art and Science.* Amsterdam: Rembrandt House Museum; Los Angeles: J. Paul Getty Museum; Zwolle: Waanders, 2008.

Schmidt-Loske, Katharina. "Historical Sketch: Maria Sibylla Merian, Metamorphosis of Insects." *Deutsche Entomologische Zeitschrift* 57 (2010): 5–10.

Siegal, Nina. "A Slice of Russia in Amsterdam." *New York Times*, May 22, 2013. http://www.nytimes.com/2013/05/23/arts/artsspecial/A-Slice-of-Russia-in-Amsterdam.html?mcubz=2.

Wettengl, Kurt, ed. *Maria Sibylla Merian, 1647–1717: Artist and Naturalist.* Ostfildern-Ruit: Verlag Gerd Hatje, 1998.

Zemon Davis, Natalie. *Women on the Margins: Three Seventeenth-Century Lives.* Cambridge, MA: Harvard University Press, 1995.

Additional primary and secondary sources may be found at http://www.themariasibyllamerian society.humanities.uva.nl

Quotations in English
Quotations from Maria Sibylla's books and letters were translated by Malcolm Davies or reprinted or adapted by the authors from the following sources (full citations are above; notes by page number can be found at www.getty.edu/education/merian).

Merian, Maria Sibylla. *Metamorphosis Insectorum Surinamensium.* Commentary by Elisabeth Rücker and William T. Stearn.

———. *Metamorphosis Insectorum Surinamensium.* Edited by Marieke van Delft and Hans Mulder. English translations by Patrick Lennon.

Reitsma, Ella. *Maria Sibylla Merian & Daughters: Women of Art and Science.*

Wettengl, Kurt, ed. *Maria Sibylla Merian, 1647–1717: Artist and Naturalist.*

Zemon Davis, Natalie. *Women on the Margins: Three Seventeenth-Century Lives.*

Index

Published by the J. Paul Getty Museum, Los Angeles
Getty Publications
1200 Getty Center Drive, Suite 500
Los Angeles, California 90049-1682
www.getty.edu/publications

Elizabeth S. G. Nicholson, *Project Editor*
Ann Hofstra Grogg, *Manuscript Editor*
Kurt Hauser, *Designer*
Victoria Gallina, *Production*

Distributed in North America by ABRAMS
Distributed outside North America by Yale University Press, London

Printed in China

Library of Congress Cataloging-in-Publication Data

Names: Pomeroy, Sarah B., author. | Kathirithamby, Jeyaraney, author. | J.
  Paul Getty Museum, issuing body.
Title: Maria Sibylla Merian : artist, scientist, adventurer / Sarah B.
  Pomeroy and Jeyaraney Kathirithamby.
Description: First edition. | Los Angeles : J. Paul Getty Museum, [2018] |
  Includes bibliographical references.
Identifiers: LCCN 2017021576 | ISBN 9781947440012 (hardcover)
Subjects: LCSH: Merian, Maria Sibylla, 1647-1717. | Women
  naturalists—Germany—Biography—Juvenile literature. | Natural history
  illustrators—Germany—Biography—Juvenile literature.
Classification: LCC QH31.M45 P66 2017 | DDC 508.092 [B] —dc23
LC record available at https://lccn.loc.gov/2017021576

Printed and bound in China by Asia Pacific Offset (JF17090016)
First printing by the J. Paul Getty Museum (13902)

Resources for readers and teachers are available free online!
www.getty.edu/education/merian